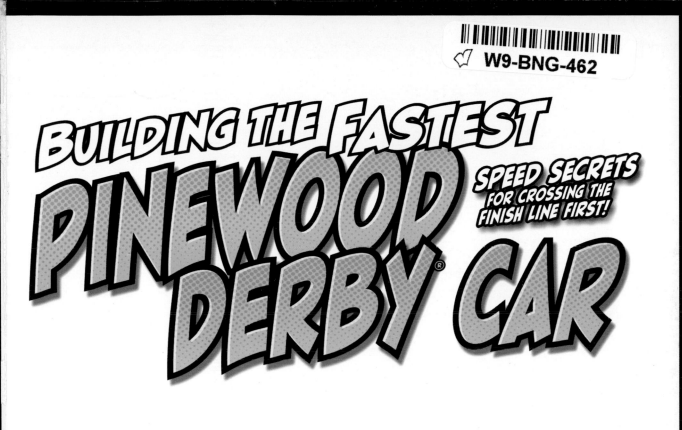

Building the Fastest Pinewood Derby Car

SPEED SECRETS FOR CROSSING THE FINISH LINE FIRST!

BUILDING THE FASTEST PINEWOOD DERBY® CAR

SPEED SECRETS FOR CROSSING THE FINISH LINE FIRST!

TROY THORNE

Fox Chapel
PUBLISHING

DEDICATION

I dedicate this book with love and thanks to my family: my wife Beth, who has stuck with me through everything, and my three children, Nathan, Kelsey, and Camryn. And, to my parents and grandfather, for teaching me to try anything. You all make it possible for me to pursue my ideas, while putting up with all the headaches of the big projects I get involved in.

ACKNOWLEDGMENTS

I'd like to thank the team at Fox Chapel Publishing for once again helping me get my ideas on to paper. Kerri Landis, for deciphering my writing and shaping it into usable text, Jason Deller for his amazing cartoon drawings of Dash and his friends, and Scott Kriner the best photographer in the world. I would also like to thank FatSebastian, Sporty and RacerX at www.derbytalk.com for their help with reviewing the technical details.

© 2012 by Troy Thorne and Fox Chapel Publishing Company, Inc., East Petersburg, PA.

Building the Fastest Pinewood Derby® Car is an original work, first published in 2012 by Fox Chapel Publishing Company, Inc. The patterns contained herein are copyrighted by the author. Readers may make copies of these patterns for personal use. The patterns themselves, however, are not to be duplicated for resale or distribution under any circumstances. Any such copying is a violation of copyright law.

Pinewood Derby®, Cub Scouts®, and Boy Scouts of America® are registered trademarks of the Boy Scouts of America. This independent model-maker's guide is not sponsored or endorsed by, or affiliated with, any of the organizations whose trademarks appear for informational purposes only.

ISBN 978-1-56523-762-9

To learn more about the other great books from Fox Chapel Publishing, or to find a retailer near you, call toll-free 800-457-9112 or visit us at *www.FoxChapelPublishing.com*.

Note to Authors: We are always looking for talented authors to write new books in our area of woodworking, design, and related crafts. Please send a brief letter describing your idea to Acquisition Editor, 1970 Broad Street, East Petersburg, PA 17520.

Printed in China
First printing

About the Author

Creative Director, woodworker, and Assistant Scoutmaster Troy Thorne has helped to build hundreds of derby cars. He participates in Scouting activities with his son, Nathan, who was a national finalist in the All-Star Derby Design Contest. Nate has grown out of Cub Scouts and is on his way to Eagle, but luckily Troy's daughter, Kelsey, is racing Awana cars. Troy's latest project is a street-legal AC Cobra replica.

Dear Adventurers,

I'd like you to meet Dash Derby. Dash, his little sister Dottie and his friends, Max Design and Professor Speed, will be your tour guides through the process of building a derby car. Dash's character is part me, and part all the kids I've worked with making hundreds of derby cars over the past twelve years. The part of him that comes from me likes red, and especially likes fast cars! Follow along with Dash and his friends and you'll be able to build a super fast derby car, too!

          - Troy

CONTENTS

COOL STUFF FOR KIDS!

HI, KIDS! I'm Dash Derby, and I'll be one of your guides through the daring world of Pinewood Derby racing. This book is designed so the larger process of building a car is split into smaller pieces. As you progress through the chapters, be sure to take your time. A good idea would be to do one part each day, or one part every few days. Set goals for yourself and stick to them—and you'll have an awesome car built in no time! Building a derby car is fun and exciting, but there are some ground rules you should follow.

Dash's Rules for Derby Adventurers

1. Have **FUN!**

2. Don't wait until the last minute to get started.

3. If you get tired, stop.

4. Don't let your parents take over—this is your project.

5. The derby isn't about winning—it's about having fun and learning new skills along the way!

BORING STUFF FOR MOM AND DAD

HI, ADULTS! If you and your child are ready to build the fastest car at the Pinewood Derby, you've come to the right place. This book will guide you through the creation of a derby car from start to finish, explaining everything you need to know.

The Pinewood Derby experience is a great way to spend quality time with your child, and to allow him to develop a sense of pride in his own work. Work as a team, and don't be afraid to give your child the reins—after all, this is his project! It's impossible for your child to fully experience the Pinewood Derby if YOU build the car. Remember—the number one goal of the Derby is having fun!

What NOT to do.

Don't find yourself in this situation. The car doesn't have to be perfect—it just needs to be your child's!

GETTING STARTED

We've broken down the process into chapters. These chapters can be approached one at a time. I recommend giving each step its own separate day; that way, your child can accomplish the tasks without getting tired. If you create a schedule of accomplishing one or two of the steps a week, you can have your car done well in advance of race day.

CHAPTER **1**

PLANNING
The first step is familiarizing yourself with the process. What tools do you need? Which science principles do you need to understand? Start on page 12.

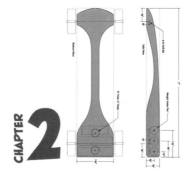

CHAPTER **2**

DESIGNING
Picking an awesome design for your Pinewood Derby car is the second step. Go to page 20 to pinpoint which design you want for your award-winning car!

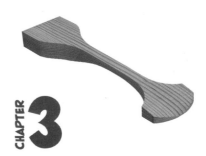

CHAPTER **3**

SHAPING
Now you're cookin'...after progressing through this chapter, your project will actually start looking like a car. See page 40.

CHAPTER 4

WEIGHTING

Properly adding weights to your car is one of the easiest things you can do to increase the speed of the car. Check out page 54 to learn more.

CHAPTER 5

FINISHING

The Finishing chapter will teach you how to make your car look super-cool. Your car will be the envy of all the other racers after this step! See page 68.

CHAPTER 6

AXLE PREP

You might think axles are boring, but if you skip this step, your car won't go fast. Be sure to pay attention to this chapter! Read from page 88 to learn how to master the axles.

CHAPTER 7

WHEEL PREP

Round wheels will help your car track more smoothly. Putting a little effort in here will have big payoffs on race day. Check out page 98.

CHAPTER 8

ASSEMBLY

Turn to page 106 to read the secrets of perfectly assembling your car. All the fine tuning and adjusting is done at this step to get your car running as fast as it can.

CHAPTER 9

RACE DAY

Your car is ready to go...now what? This chapter explains everything you need to know about race day. See page 128.

PLANNING

Hi everyone! I'm Dash Derby, and this is my little sister, Dottie. This chapter teaches you to plan the best derby car. It's the starting line on your way to derby car greatness!

You don't start creating a Pinewood Derby car by jumping right in and starting to cut away wood. You must first understand the principles of speed before you can apply them. I've been asked many times what the secret is to building a fast car. I always reply the same way—there is no magic "one" thing you can do to make your car faster. It is a combination of a lot of different things that all add up to a very fast car. Some things are more important than others—keep reading to find out more.

BUILDING A CAR TOGETHER

Spending time with your child is one of the most rewarding aspects of participating in the Pinewood Derby. Also, pay close attention to what you and your child can learn from building a car together. Though some may seem obvious, following a few simple principles will help make the Pinewood Derby a truly rewarding experience for both of you.

WORK AS A TEAM.

Find a way for your child to participate in every step of the process. The best way to accomplish this is to let him perform as many steps as possible. Teach by example whenever you can. For instance, you might show your child how to complete a step of the process on one side of the car and then allow him, to do the same step on the other side of the car. If he is unable to complete the step by himself, assist him but be sure he participates as much as possible. Some steps must be performed by an adult for safety reasons. Even in these situations, try to find some way to safely involve your child in the work you do.

Whether or not he can perform a particular step, encourage your child to work closely by your side so he can see exactly what you are doing. You may want to provide something safe for him to stand on so he can be at your eye level. Ask questions, such as "Do both sides look even?" to help keep him focused on the task even if he isn't physically doing the work. The more steps your child understands and participates in, the more he will feel as if he is a part of the process.

LET YOUR CHILD DECIDE THE CAR DESIGN.

Your child will feel more connected to his car if you allow him to be creative and influence its design. This book provides several patterns for all skill levels. Look through the designs with your child and decide on one together. Consider the level of woodworking experience needed before you commit to building a specific car.

LET YOUR CHILD PICK THE COLOR AND DETAIL OPTIONS.

If he wants to add detail, such as stickers, or decals, encourage him to express his creativity in this area. Allow him to place them on the car. Putting your child in charge of different aspects of the project shows him that you value his judgment.

TEACH SKILLS AND TECHNIQUES AS YOU WORK.

Building a Pinewood Derby car with your child is a great way to develop woodworking, math, and science skills. Go over all of the tools and their uses with your child and help him understand how they work. When it's time to actually build the car, remember to teach by example and to allow your child to learn at his own pace. You might show him how to hold the coping saw and then let him make the cuts on the car by imitating the position and techniques you've demonstrated. Always encourage your child: Be quick with praise and downplay small mistakes.

MAKE IT FUN.

The Pinewood Derby is a great opportunity for you and your child to create a special bond as you work together to build the car. Give yourself enough time so you and your child don't feel rushed or overwhelmed. Remember, building a Pinewood Derby car should be a fun experience for both of you.

Don't forget to pick up a can of elbow grease!

elbow grease

NET WT. 4 OZ

SAFETY

Safety is the number one tool in your bag of tricks. Always be mindful of your fingers and body parts to avoid injuries—make sure that your fingers are not in the path of a saw blade or sanding pad. There are a few pieces of safety equipment that will help you: a dust mask, safety glasses, and ear protection.

Wear a dust mask to protect against airborne particles when you're sanding, applying graphite, and spray painting. Form the metal strip at the top of the mask over your nose to create a tight seal.

Always wear eye protection when sanding wood and working with power tools. Wear some safety glasses or goggles to make sure no stray bits of wood or metal fillings find their way into your eyes.

Power drills, band saws, and sanders can be noisy. If the noise bothers your child, you'll want to use ear protection like earplugs or headphone-style ear muffs.

About Lead

Lead is a soft, dense metal often recommended for derby cars. However, lead is toxic and could harm your health if it gets inside your body. Do not touch your mouth or face while working with lead. Clean up your work area and tools after lead is used, and be sure to thoroughly wash your hands, skin, and clothes. Do not sand or grind lead because the dust is hard to clean up and might be inhaled. Melting hot lead is dangerous.

Safety Glasses.

Dust Mask.

Ear Protection.

WORKSPACE

If you have a workshop in the garage or basement, that is a fantastic spot to build a derby car. If not, the kitchen or picnic table is just as good. If you're not working in a designated shop area, just make sure to cover your work surface with newspaper.

DERBY WORKSHOP

Most Cub Scout packs have a Derby Workshop in the weeks before the Derby. It is a great idea to take advantage of this if you are interested in learning how to use cool tools—like band saws, scroll saws, power drills, and power sanders—with the help of someone experienced.

This way, you can also avoid needing to purchase power tools if you don't have much other use for them. Plus, it's always fun to work on your car with other kids; you never know who will have a great idea to volunteer.

Above: In the photo, my daughter and I are building a car for her Awana derby race.

Pinewood Derby isn't just for boys anymore!

Girls complete in derbies held by church organizations such as Awana®. Brownie Girl Scout® troops also hold Powder Puff Derbies. The rules are basically the same, but the cars look different. The girls' cars tend to be pink and purple with hearts and kittens on them.

ANATOMY OF A DERBY CAR

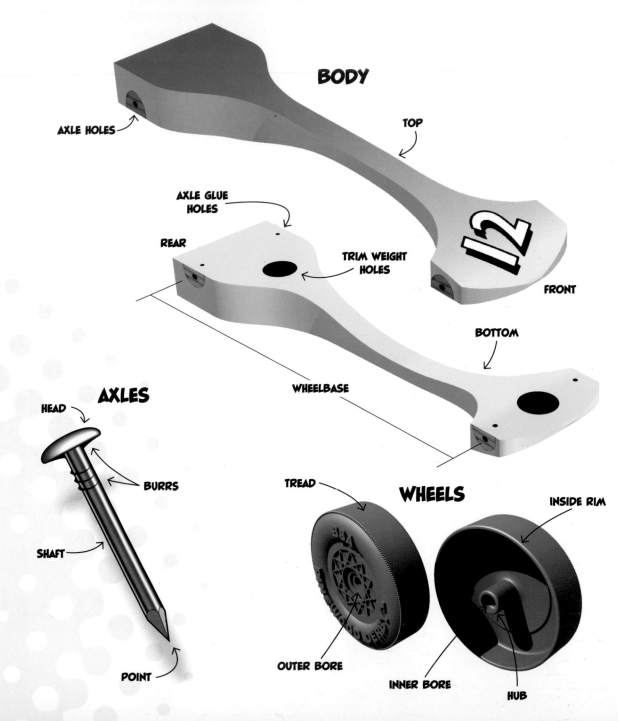

BODY

AXLE HOLES

TOP

AXLE GLUE HOLES

REAR

TRIM WEIGHT HOLES

FRONT

BOTTOM

WHEELBASE

12

AXLES

HEAD

BURRS

SHAFT

POINT

WHEELS

TREAD

INSIDE RIM

OUTER BORE

INNER BORE

HUB

RULES

As you gather the tools and materials for the building process, review the official and local Pinewood Derby rules and the Official Grand Prix Pinewood Derby car specifications. The list of suggested rules that accompanies each Official Grand Prix Pinewood Derby Kit® is shown at right and the size specifications are illustrated below. If you don't have a copy of your local rules, ask your local race committee for one. Then abide by all of them. Remember, when you compete in the Pinewood Derby, be honest. If one of the designs or techniques in this book does not fit within your local Derby's rules, don't use it. If you are unsure whether something is legal, check with your local race organizer before you build the car.

OFFICIAL PINEWOOD DERBY RULES

1 Wheel bearings and bushings are prohibited.

2 The car shall not ride on springs.

3 Only official Cub Scout Grand Prix Pinewood Derby wheels and axles are permitted.

4 Only dry lubricant is permitted.

5 Details, such as steering wheel and driver, are permissible as long as these details do not exceed the maximum length, width, and weight specifications.

6 The car must be free-wheeling, with no starting devices.

7 Each car must pass inspection, the owner will be informed of the reason for failure, and will be given time within the official weigh-in time period to make the adjustment.

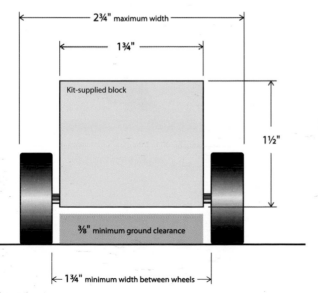

2¾" maximum width

1¾"

Kit-supplied block

1½"

⅜" minimum ground clearance

1¾" minimum width between wheels

The speed of a car can be directly related to three basic things: the placement of the weight in the car, reduction of friction, and the alignment of the wheels. If you can get those three principles nailed down, your car will be faster than greased lightning.

> Greetings readers, I'm Professor Speed. In this section, you'll learn how to manipulate the three core principles of speed to make your car the fastest one on the track!

PRINCIPLE 1:

WEIGHT PLACEMENT

Gravity provides the energy that makes your car roll down the track. Before the race begins, your car is sitting stationary at the top of the track. It isn't moving yet. At this time, your car has what is called potential energy. Potential energy is the amount of energy available to make your car roll down the track.

To maximize the potential energy stored in your car, you want the weight far in the back and low in the car. But, at the same time, you don't want too much weight in the back, causing your car to pop wheelies down the track. You want your car to have a balance point, or center of gravity, in front of the rear axle. On smooth metal tracks, you want the balance point to be $3/4$" in front of the rear axle. On rougher wooden tracks, it's safer to set it at 1." Use trim weights to adjust the center of balance. See page 67.

The reasons for having the weight in the back are very simple. All the cars start at the same height on the track. But, a car with its weight in the back will have higher potential energy because the weight has farther to travel to reach the ground. It's like having a bigger engine with higher horsepower under the hood.

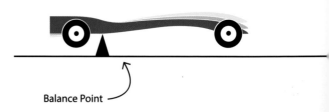

Balance Point

PRINCIPLE 2:

REDUCE FRICTION

More friction equals less speed. You might have built a car that has lots of potential energy, but not all of that energy converts into speed. Some energy changes into heat when surfaces, like the wheel and the axle, or the wheel and the track, rub against each other. This is friction. If you can cut down on this waste of the car's potential energy, you will increase your speed.

Below are the main areas of friction:

☐ Inside rim of the wheels striking the track guides as the car travels down the track

☐ Wheel surface riding down the track

☐ Wheel bore rotating on the axle shafts

☐ Wheels rubbing on the axle heads

☐ Wheel hubs rubbing the side of the car

☐ Friction against the air as the car moves down the track

PRINCIPLE 3:

WHEEL ALIGNMENT

If you maximize all the potential energy, polish the wheels and axles to reduce all the friction, and then just stick the wheels on your car, you will be very surprised how poorly your car will preform. If your car travels down the track and bounces off the guide rail a few times, it will be losing speed every time it touches the rail. Or, your alignment may be so far off that your car will get the "death wobble," where the back of the car wobbles back and forth. I've seen very fast cars start the "death wobble" as soon as the car hits the flat part of the track, and it looks like the car put on its brakes. A finely aligned car will look like it's accelerating down the flat part of the track. What's really happening is an aligned car isn't losing as much speed as the unaligned cars.

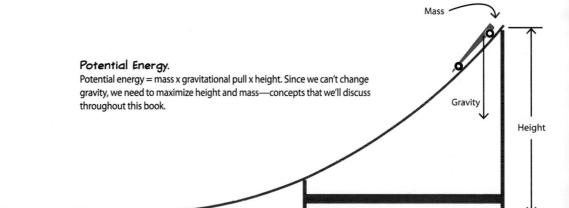

Potential Energy.
Potential energy = mass x gravitational pull x height. Since we can't change gravity, we need to maximize height and mass—concepts that we'll discuss throughout this book.

DESIGNING

Hey there—I'm Max Design. I'll help you pick out a cool style for your car.

There are endless choices when you are designing a Pinewood Derby car. You can build racecars, buses, cars shaped like hot dogs, or even pencils; you are only limited by your own imagination. You'll be amazed by all the creative ideas you see at the Pinewood Derby races you attend.

To build a speedy car, it is best to stick with simpler designs that maximize all the design points we will discuss in this chapter.

Remember to include your child in the design discussions and decisions. Use the design process as an opportunity to teach your child about these design principles.

GENERAL GUIDELINES FOR CAR DESIGN

DIMENSIONS

The dimensions of your car must remain within the width, height, length, and weight specifications listed in your Derby rules. The official Boy Scouts of America (BSA®) specifications are outlined on page 17 of this book. You don't want to make your car shorter than the maximum length. A shorter car's weight won't be as high on the track as a longer car, lowering the potential energy. So stick with car designs that use the total length of the block of wood.

LOW-PROFILE DESIGN

Aerodynamics play a smaller role in Pinewood Derby racing than they do in full-size automobile racing. The best approach is to make your design as "low profile," or as thin, as possible. This will give you two advantages; First, the car will be very aerodynamic, and second, the car body will weigh very little so you can move even more weight to the rear of the car. Simpler car designs can get as thin as $\frac{1}{4}$" and not break in a race.

ROUND FRONT

Avoid any designs that don't have flat or slightly rounded front shapes. Cars with a narrow pointy nose will never sit against the starting pin and may get disqualified from the race. Also, any car that has a slot cut into the front of it that allows part of the car past the starting pin might get disqualified.

WEIGHT AREA

Placing the weights in the rear of the car requires that you design the car to have enough room to fit in all the weight needed to get the car to 5.0 ounces. The type of weights you choose will determine how much room you will need. Tungsten is the densest type of weight and will require the least space to install. Lead will require over a third more space to achieve the same weight as tungsten. In chapter 3, I've explained the different types of weights available and recommendations for the placement in the car.

EXTENDED WHEELBASE

If your rules allow the wheelbase to be changed from the supplied slots in the block of wood, it's best to extend the wheelbase as wide as you can (without the wheel treads extending past the ends of the car). This helps your car in many ways, you can put the weight all the way to the back and still have perfect center of balance.

FLAT BOTTOM

If your pack's track uses a ramp braking area at the end of the track, you may want to consider a design with a flat bottom. If your design has an arch between the wheels, your speedy car will have far less area making contact with the rubber strips on the braking ramps. My son has had his speed car flip off the end of the track and roll under the spectator's chairs. Never a good thing for the wheel alignment!

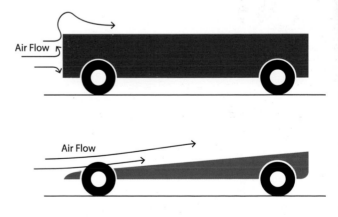

Aerodynamic Designs.
An aerodynamic design allows the air to move over and around the car body in a smooth manner. The most basic aerodynamic design is the simple wedge (bottom).

WEDGE-A-MATIC

STANDARD & EXTENDED WHEELBASE

APPROXIMATE WEIGHT
Body Weight – 2.3 oz
Body, Wheels & Axles Weight – 2.8 oz

RECOMMENDED MAIN WEIGHT OPTIONS
Lead Wire
Tungsten Cylinders
Tungsten Slotted disc
Tungsten Cubes

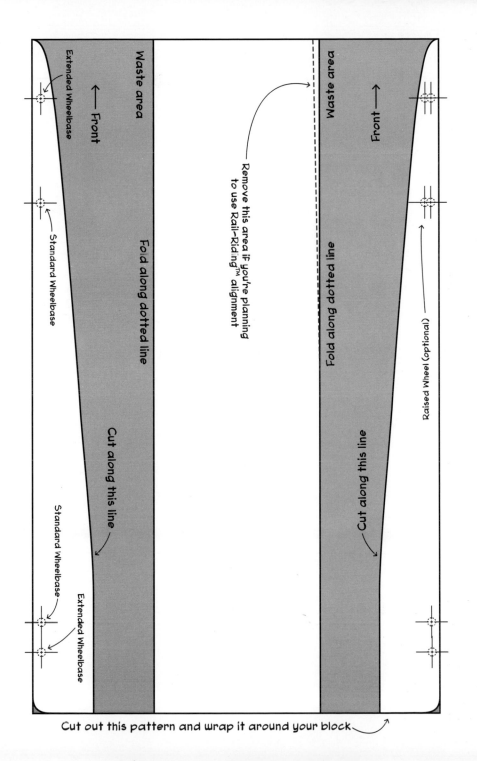

Cut out this pattern and wrap it around your block

23

THE LOWDOWN

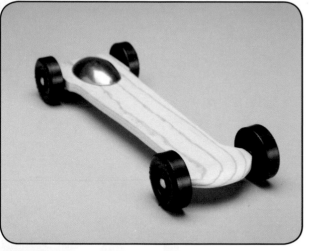

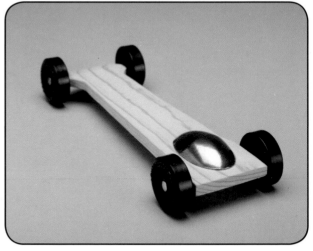

APPROXIMATE WEIGHT
Body Weight – 0.6 oz
Body, Wheels & Axles Weight – 1.1 oz

RECOMMENDED MAIN WEIGHT OPTIONS
Tungsten Canopy (3.5 oz)
Tungsten Cubes

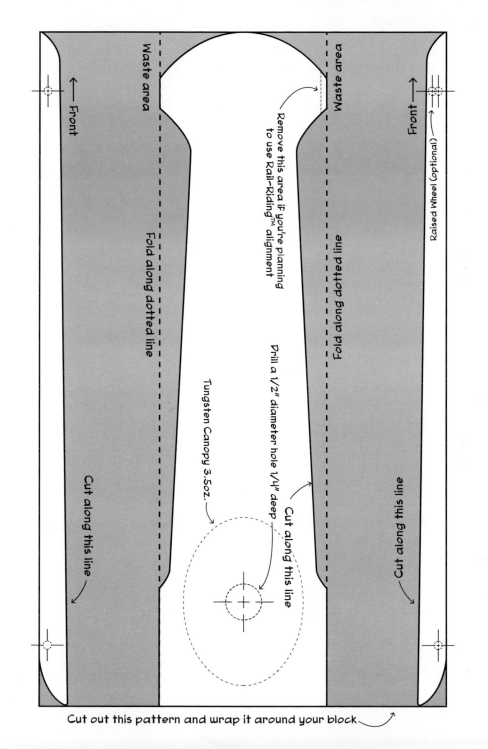

Waste area

← Front

Fold along dotted line

Cut along this line

Remove this area if you're planning to use Rail-Riding™ alignment

Drill a 1/2" diameter hole 1/4" deep

Tungsten Canopy 3.5oz.

Cut along this line

Waste area

Fold along dotted line

Front →

Raised Wheel (optional)

Cut along this line

Cut out this pattern and wrap it around your block

SPEED SWOOP

APPROXIMATE WEIGHT
Body Weight - 0.7 oz
Body, Wheels & Axles Weight - 1.2 oz

RECOMMENDED MAIN WEIGHT OPTIONS
Lead Wire
Tungsten Cylinders
Tungsten Slotted disc
Tungsten Cubes

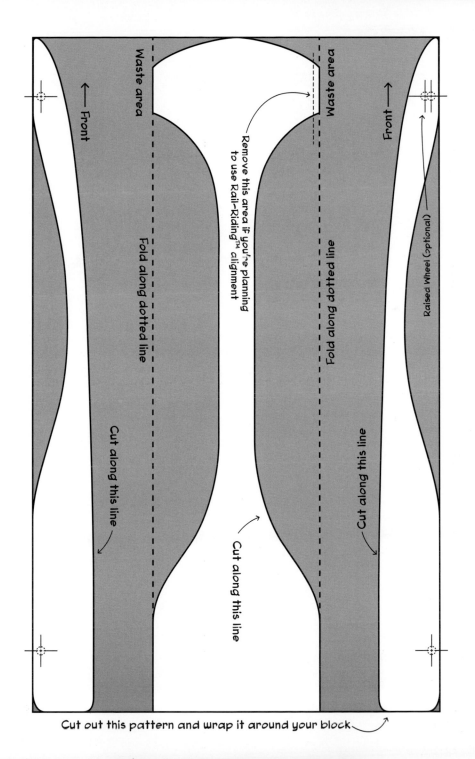

Cut out this pattern and wrap it around your block

Building the Fastest **PINEWOOD DERBY CAR**

WONDER WIGGLE

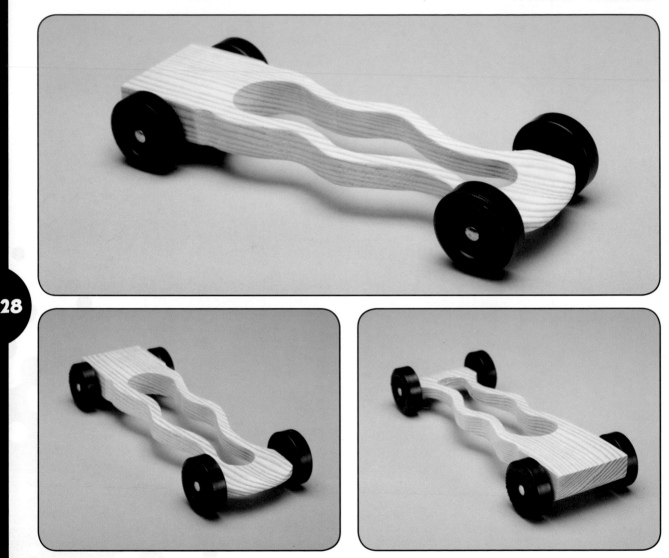

APPROXIMATE WEIGHT
Body Weight – 0.9 oz
Body, Wheels & Axles Weight – 1.4 oz

RECOMMENDED MAIN WEIGHT OPTIONS
Lead Wire
Tungsten Cylinders
Tungsten Slotted disc
Tungsten Cubes

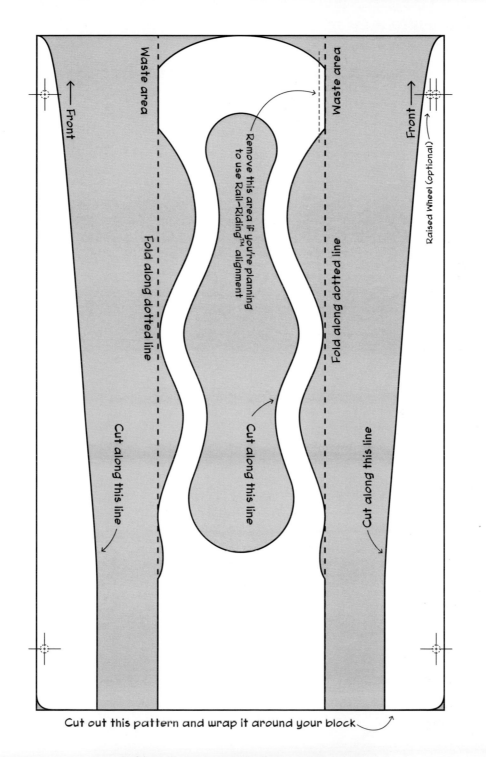

Cut out this pattern and wrap it around your block

WIDE OPEN

APPROXIMATE WEIGHT
Body Weight - 0.8 oz
Body, Wheels & Axles Weight - 1.3 oz

RECOMMENDED MAIN WEIGHT OPTIONS
Lead Wire
Tungsten Cylinders
Tungsten Slotted disc
Tungsten Cubes

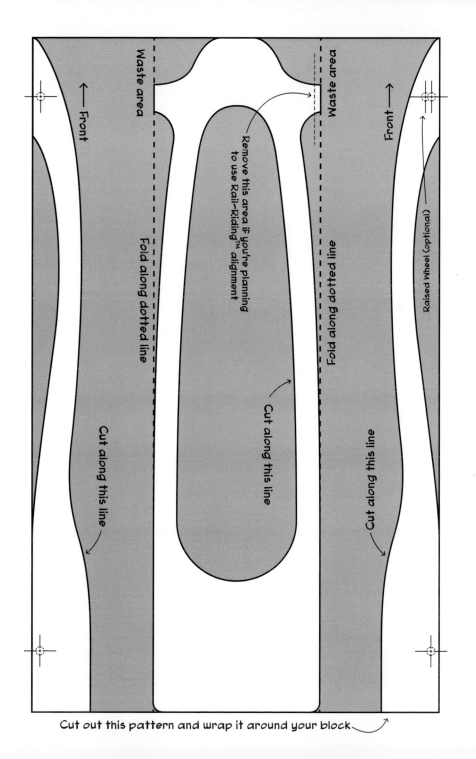

Waste area

Front →

Fold along dotted line

Cut along this line

Remove this area if you're planning to use Rail-Riding™ alignment

Cut along this line

Waste area

← Front

Fold along dotted line

Raised Wheel (optional)

Cut along this line

Cut out this pattern and wrap it around your block

DESIGNING

SOLE-RUNNER

APPROXIMATE WEIGHT
Body Weight – 1.1 oz
Body, Wheels & Axles Weight – 1.6 oz

RECOMMENDED MAIN WEIGHT OPTIONS
Lead Wire
Tungsten Cylinders
Tungsten Slotted disc
Tungsten Cubes
Tungsten Canopy

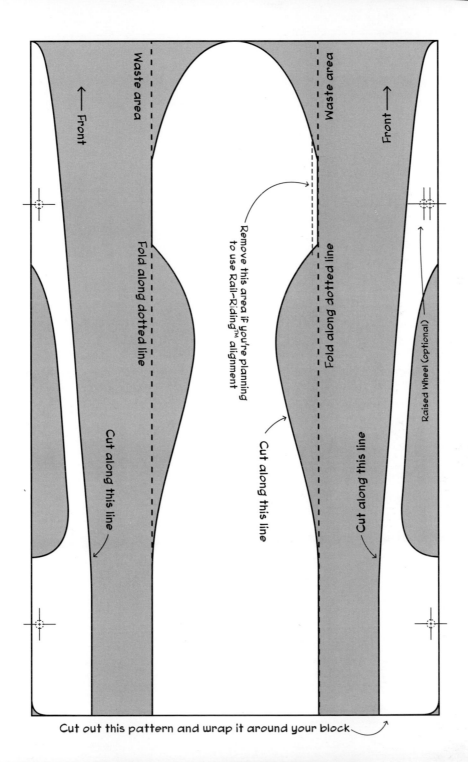

Waste area

← Front

Front →

Waste area

Fold along dotted line

Fold along dotted line

Remove this area if you're planning
to use Rail-Riding™ alignment

Cut along this line

Cut along this line

Cut along this line

Raised Wheel (optional)

Cut out this pattern and wrap it around your block

QUICK COMET

34

APPROXIMATE WEIGHT
Body Weight – 1.1 oz
Body, Wheels & Axles Weight – 1.6 oz

RECOMMENDED MAIN WEIGHT OPTIONS
Lead Wire
Tungsten Cylinders
Tungsten Slotted disc
Tungsten Cubes

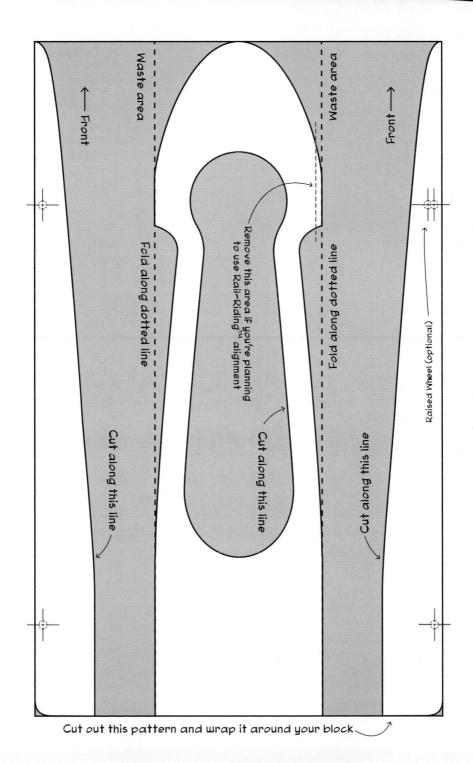

Waste area

← Front

Fold along dotted line

Cut along this line

Remove this area if you're planning to use Rail-Riding™ alignment

Cut along this line

Waste area

Front →

Fold along dotted line

Cut along this line

Raised Wheel (optional)

Cut out this pattern and wrap it around your block

OPEN ENDED

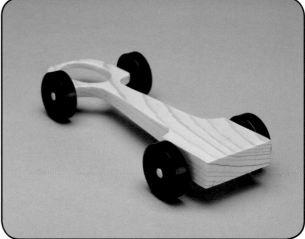

APPROXIMATE WEIGHT
Body Weight – 0.7 oz
Body, Wheels & Axles Weight – 1.2 oz

RECOMMENDED MAIN WEIGHT OPTIONS
Lead Wire
Tungsten Cylinders
Tungsten Slotted disc
Tungsten Cubes

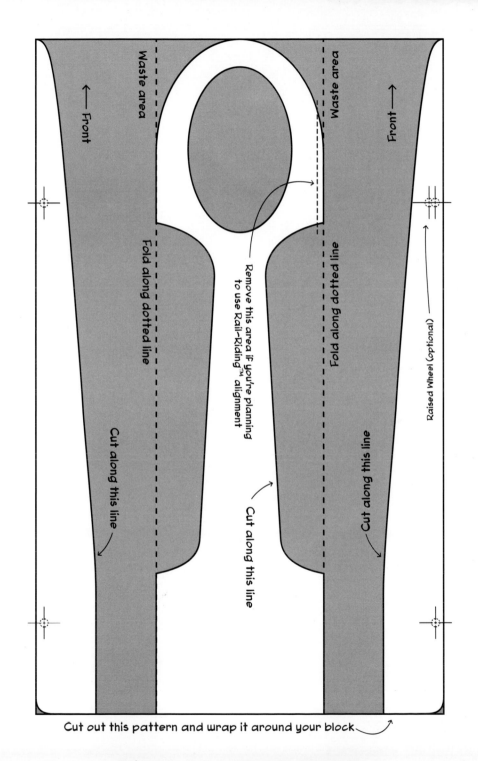

Waste area

← Front

Front →

Waste area

Fold along dotted line

Fold along dotted line

Remove this area if you're planning
to use Rail-Riding™ alignment

Cut along this line

Cut along this line

Cut along this line

Raised Wheel (optional)

Cut out this pattern and wrap it around your block

BLANK PATTERNS

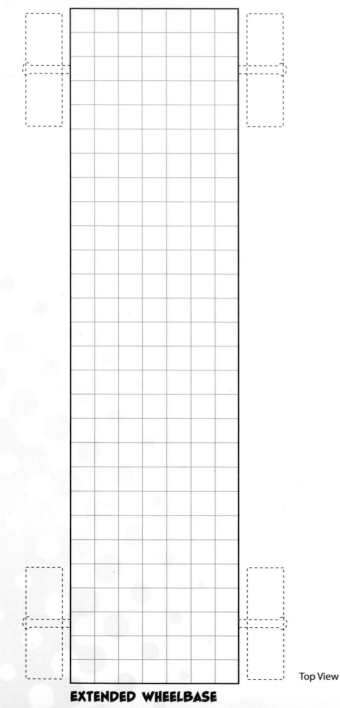

EXTENDED WHEELBASE

Top View

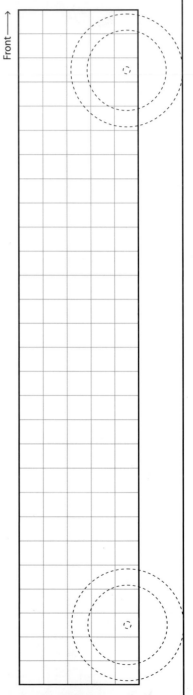

Front⟶

Side View

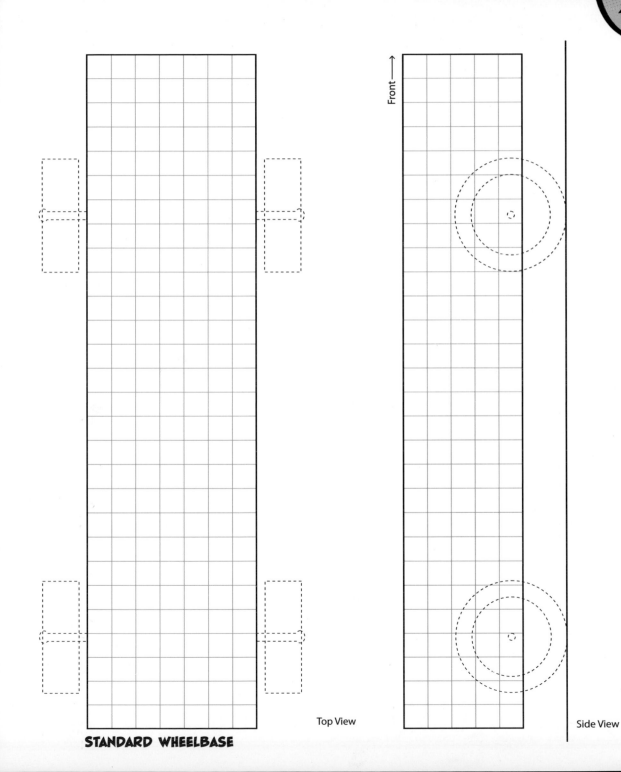

Front⟶

Top View

Side View

STANDARD WHEELBASE

SHAPING

Now that you've picked a design, you get to start shaping that block of wood! Just remember, go slowly, because you can't add wood back on!

In this chapter, we will transform your wood from the basic block to a car body that will rocket past the other cars. Before we start to cut the main shape of the car, it's a good idea to work on how the axles are going to attach. It's easier to work on a full block of wood than a very thin profile. Take your time: the better you prepare your car body, the easier it will be to attach the axles and wheels and to get the alignment correct.

TOOL OVERVIEW

On this page are some of the tools we will be using in this chapter. The options you choose for your car will determine what tools you will need. Please read though the complete chapter before you remove the first chip of wood.

SANDING BLOCKS

PENCIL

SANDPAPER

COPING SAW

EMERY BOARDS

COMBINATION SQUARE

DRILL BITS

BAND SAW

SCROLL SAW

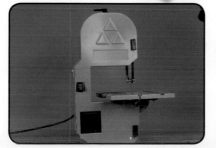

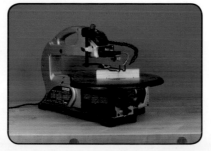

PREPPING THE AXLE SLOTS

Your wooden block has slots cut into the bottom to install the axles. If your rules require you to use these slots, it is best to prepare them as shown on this page. During your final alignment steps, you need to be able to easily remove and reinstall your axle in the same spot. Installing axles into the basic slots is very difficult; this technique makes it very simple. If you're not required to use the axle slots, drill new axle holes on the other side of the block.

1 Gather your materials.
You will need five-minute epoxy, a #44 drill bit, four extra axles, painter's tape, a Popsicle stick, and your wooden block.

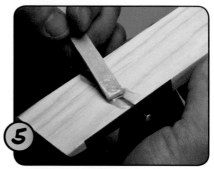

2 Pre-drill the slots.
Mount a #44 drill bit into a drill press with a squared table. Carefully ream out the slot using the top of the slot as a guide. #44 drill bits are available online or at well-stocked hardware stores.

3 Gluing the slots.
Cover the ends of the slots with painters tape. Square one end of a Popsicle stick and sand it thinner so it fits into the axle slot. Mix a small amount of 5-min epoxy and coat the bottom of the slot.

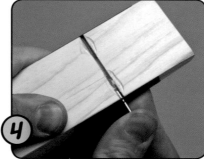

4 Inserting the axles.
Push an axle though the painters tape and into the slot. Allow ⅜" of the axle to protrude from the side of the car. Take your time and get the axles perfectly level with the bottom of the car.

5 Coating the axle.
After you're happy with the axle placement, apply more epoxy to the top of the axle and completely cover the axle. Note: don't coat the entire axle if your rules require the axle tips to be visible.

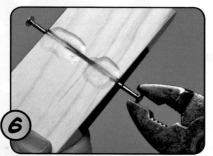

6 Removing the axle.
Allow the epoxy an hour or two to completely dry. Grab the axle head with a pair of pliers, twist the axle and pull it free. Discard the axles; the pliers will ruin the axle head in the process of removing them.

7 Sanding the bottom.
Sand the epoxy completely flat on the bottom and then remove the painter's tape.

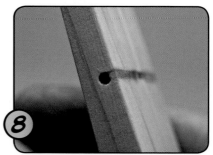

8 Final axle hole.
No more slots… you will now have perfect axle holes, just like you drilled them.

I want to thank Ryan Johnson (Sporty) for this great technique.

42

DRILLING EXTENDED AXLE HOLES

If your rules allow changing the wheelbase of your car, it is helpful to move the wheels as far apart as possible. This will give you the ability to move more weight to the rear of your car.

Drill Bit	Decimal Conversion
5/64"	0.0781"
#44	0.0860"
3/32"	0.0938"

1 Gather your materials.
You will need a square, a pencil, #44 drill bit and your block of wood. #44 drill bits are available online or at specialty fastener stores.

2 Mark the location for the holes.
Measure ⅝" from the block's front and draw a square line. Repeat for the rear. Next, measure ⅛" from the bottom to mark the axle hole.

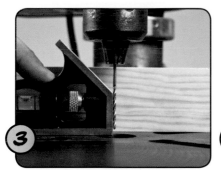

3 Squaring your drill press table.
Use a square to set your drill press table to be perfectly 90 degrees to the drill bit.

4 Guide block.
Line up the first hole and clamp a piece of wood to the drill press table behind the block. This will act as guide, ensuring all four holes will be the exact same distance from the bottom of the car.

5 Drill the holes.
With the guide block in place, it's very easy to drill the remaining holes. If you have many blocks to drill, place a pencil mark on the guide block and align the next block to those marks.

43

TIP THREE WHEELS ARE FASTER THAN FOUR

Friction is the enemy of speed! By drilling one of the front axle holes higher than the other side by 1/16", you will lift one of the front wheels off the track. This will reduce the energy needed to accelerate the car. With your car properly aligned, you won't even notice the raised wheel.

If you're using the slots in the bottom of the car, just make the slot 1/16" deeper on one side.

Raised 1/16" from the surface of the track

THE DERBY WORX PRO BODY TOOL

If you don't have a drill press, you might consider using the Derby Worx Pro Body Tool to drill perfectly aligned axle holes using your handheld power drill. The required #44 drill bit is included with the tool.

1 Test-fit the tool on the bottom of the block with the two "ears" positioned on the sides.

2 If the tool will not fit onto the block, use coarse grit sandpaper to reduce the width of the block until the tool fits snugly.

3 If the tool is loose, tighten the fit by placing a piece of paper—folded as needed—between one "ear" of the tool and the block.

4 Measure and mark the position of the new axle holes. You can use a square to draw a straight line starting at the middle of the axle slot and extending to the top of the car.

5 Position the tool on the bottom of the car with the two ears on the sides of the block. Align the index mark on the tool with the line corresponding to the rear axle slot or hole on the block. Clamp the tool in place.

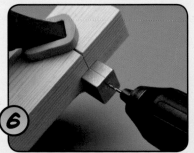

6 Hold the block firmly, position the drill bit in the hole, and slowly drill ¾" into the block. Without releasing the clamp, turn the tool and block over, and drill the second hole on the other side.

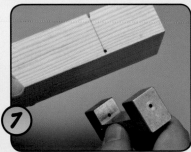

7 Repeat these steps for the other holes in the block.

Bottom of the block

8 You can use this tool to drill a raised front wheel. Transfer the line on the side of the block to the bottom of the block. Align the tool with this line, clamp it in place, and drill through the hole in the bottom of the tool.

ATTACHING THE PATTERN

Transferring the design to the block of wood can be difficult. Follow the steps on this page for the easiest way to get the design onto the block of wood.

You will need to make a photocopy of the pattern you selected from the Designing chapter, or make a copy of your own design.

The patterns in this book wrap around the top and both sides of the block of wood. I designed the patterns this way so you can refer to both sides while you're cutting along the lines of the pattern. You must saw a perfect 90-degree cut though the block. You don't want one side of the car thicker than the other side.

As you cut away parts of the block of wood, you will be removing parts of the pattern also. Simply reattach the trimmed piece of wood with clear tape so you can see the complete pattern.

Gather your materials.
You will need your wooden block, a copy of the pattern of your choice, a pair of scissors, and a glue stick or spray adhesive.

Trim the pattern.
Trim the pattern along the solid black line.. If you drilled new axle holes, attached the pattern with the slots facing up. If you're using the slots, attach the pattern with the slots facing down.

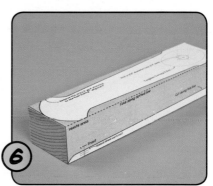

Align the pattern.
Align the pattern on the top of the block using the dotted folding lines as reference.

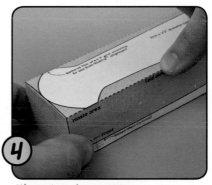

Wrapping the pattern.
Use your finger to crease the pattern along the dotted line the length of the block.

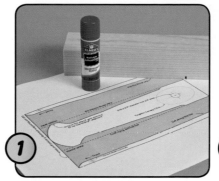

Gluing the pattern.
Remove the pattern and use a glue stick to spread a thin layer of glue on the bottom of the pattern.

Attach the pattern.
Place the pattern on the top of the block and then wrap the pattern down the sides. Be sure to not allow any wrinkles in the pattern.

45

PATTERNS ON THIN DESIGNS

On very thin cars, sometimes it can be easier to cut the block in two steps. First, attach the side pattern to the block and saw along the pattern lines. Then, use 100-grit sandpaper to remove the sawing lines from the top of the car. Finally, attach the top pattern and saw along the pattern lines.

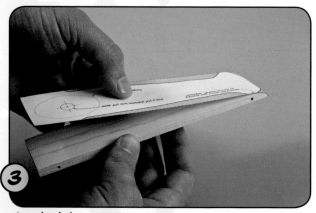

Cutting the top pattern design.
In the photo above, the side profile has already been cut from the block and sanded smooth.

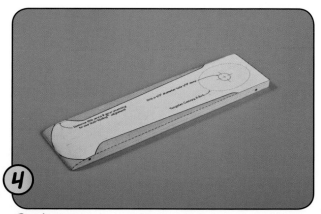

Gluing the pattern.
Use a glue stick to spread a thin coating of glue over the entire pattern.

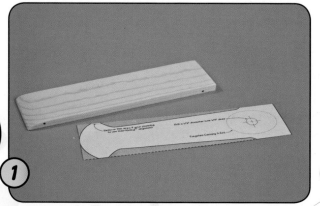

Attached the pattern.
Align the pattern to the front of the car first, and then carefully place the remainder of the pattern on the car avoiding any wrinkles.

Ready to saw.
This is what your car will look like before you saw out the final shapes.

46

DRILLING AXLE GLUE HOLES

After you drill axle holes into your car, you need to drill small holes to lock in your axles. After you get the alignment perfect, you don't want your axles to move. Also, on the track, fast cars often hit very hard at the end of the braking areas. Simple white glue will work fine to hold your axles in place.

Locate the holes.
Use the drawing below and mark the locations of the glue holes.

Drilling the holes.
Use a ⅟₁₆" or #44 drill bit and drill a hole though the bottom of the car and into the axle slot. Be sure to stop the drill when you hit the axle hole.

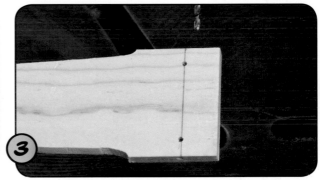

Repeat for the next three holes.
Clean out both the glue holes and the axle holes of any loose drill shavings.

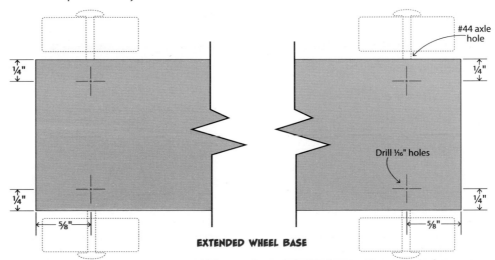

¼"

¼"

¼"

¼"

#44 axle hole

Drill ⅟₁₆" holes

⅝"

⅝"

EXTENDED WHEEL BASE

WEIGHT TRIM HOLES

Weight trim holes are used to add the last little bit of weight to get your car up to maximum weight. The shallow holes give you the perfect location to add tungsten putty or lead split shot. I use a ½" drill bit, but any large drill bit will work. The placement will depend on the type of weight you're using. Refer to diagrams on pages 57 to 65 for the location of the rear hole. Drill the front hole 1" back from the front edge of the car. If possible, make the rear hole deeper than the front. Most of the added weight will go into the rear hole. The front hole is to adjust the center of balance of the car.

Setting up to drill.
Transfer the guidelines to the bottom of the car. Use a piece of wood to get your car bottom close to level with the drill press surface. I've shown this process using a drill press, but a hand-held drill will also work.

Drilling the rear hole.
Once you have your car level, slowly drill into the car body. The slower you drill, the cleaner the hole will be. Drill the hole about ¼" deep.

Drilling the front hole.
Follow the same procedure as the rear hole but don't drill as deep. A ⅛" hole will be fine. Be very careful not to accidently drill though the front of the car.

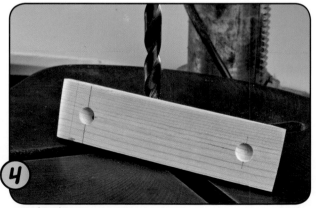

Final holes.
Clean any wood chips from the holes.

COPING SAW SKILLS

THE STRAIGHT CUT

Using a coping saw is a fun way for you to remove wood from the block yourself. Make sure you read the next few pages carefully before you pick up a saw. After you understand how to use a coping saw, you can make your car any shape you want! The first step is learning how to do a straight cut. If you have trouble getting the saw started, make a few short cuts at first—don't try to use the whole length of the saw blade.

Make a mark.
Mark the point where you want the straight line to be. Use a ruler to make a straight line where your mark is.

Prepare the vise.
Use painter's tape to stick a thin piece of scrap wood to both jaws of the vise. This will prevent crunching the piece you're cutting.

Clamp the wood.
Place the wood between the jaws of the vise and gently tighten the vise until the wood is secure. Be sure to leave a few inches of space between the cutting path and the vise.

Cut the line.
Hold the saw handle with your dominant hand. Use your other hand to hold the piece steady, or to guide the other end of the saw. Keep the saw blade level and straight from the front to the back.

TIP USING POWER TOOLS

Band Saw
Small benchtop band saws are great for cutting out Pinewood Derby cars. A fine ⅛" blade produces the best results. Provide a secure platform that's a safe distance away from the front of the saw so your child can watch you cut and see how the saw works.

Scroll Saw
Scroll saws are perfect for Pinewood Derby cars because their fine blades cut very tight curves; however, they can only cut wood less than 2½" thick. Remember to find a safe spot for your child to stand and watch.

Band Saws.
Band saws are great for cutting straight lines and curves. The only things you can't cut are internal shapes.

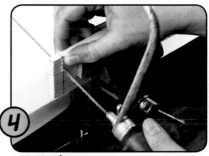

Scroll Saws.
Scroll saws are easy for kids to use. The speed can be slowed down, making it easier for kids to control the cutting.

COPING SAW SKILLS

THE CURVED CUT

Making a curved cut with the coping saw is pretty similar to making a straight cut. You still need to pay attention, go slowly, and keep the saw blade straight through the entire cut. The biggest difference is you're likely to need to move the hoop of the saw out of the way. Luckily, that is pretty easy—coping saws have a twist fastener that lets you orient the blade however you want.

1

Clamp the wood.
Put the piece of wood between the jaws of the vise so you can get to the area you need to cut.

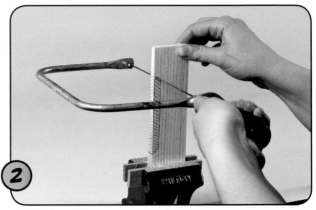

2

Start the cut.
When you get to a spot where you can't saw without hitting the hoop of the saw on the wood, remove the saw from the cut.

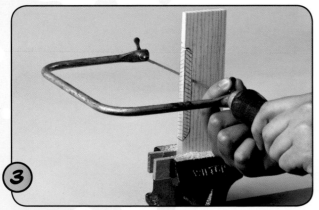

3

Move the hoop.
Loosen the blade and twist the hoop so it's out of the way. Retighten the blade and continue sawing.

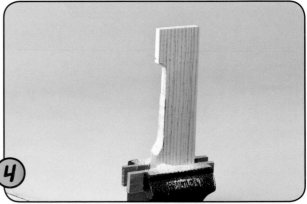

4

Finish the cut.
Keep sawing until you've finished your cut. If you need to readjust the hoop again, stop and do it.

50

COPING SAW SKILLS

THE INTERNAL CUT

An internal cut is when you cut out a shape that is completely surrounded by wood. It is a hole through the car. It's a cool-looking effect that doesn't take much more effort than making a straight cut—you just have to have your mom or dad help you drill to get started.

1

Drill an entry hole.
Drill an entry hole near the outline of the shape.

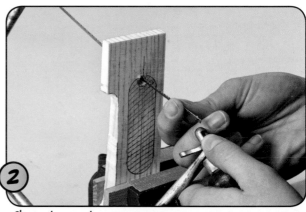

2

Clamp the wood.
Unfasten the blade and poke it through the hole in the wood. Hook up the blade to the saw again, and you're ready to go!

3

Saw on the lines.
Follow the lines you drew and cut out the piece.

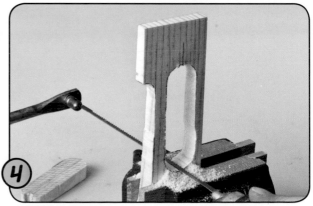

4

Knock out the piece.
When you have cut the whole way around, poke out the piece with your finger.

SHAPING WITH POWER!

Using a rotary carving tool, such as the Dremel shown here, is a great way to make your car even cooler, and it's faster than sanding by hand. However, you don't need to do this—elbow grease and sandpaper is all you really need. Make sure you're wearing a dust mask and ear protection.

Useful Dremel Bits

¼" Sanding Drum   ½" Sanding Drum   Tungsten Carbide Cutter   Dremel Chuck

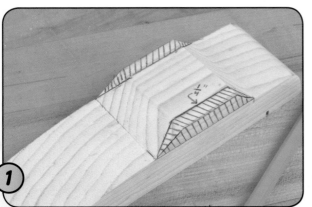

1

Marking the car.
A Dremel will remove wood very fast. Before I turn on the Dremel, I like to plan ahead and mark the areas that I want to remove.

2

Work around the axle area.
Don't remove any wood around the axle slots or holes. You want these areas to remain flat and square to the bottom of the car.

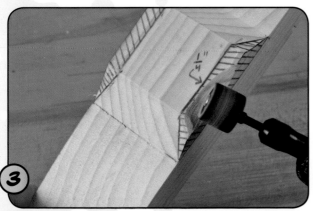

3

Using the Dremel.
Select the bit that you want to use. Turn the Dremel on to medium speed. Slowing remove the material in many light passes.

4

Final sanding
Use 220 sandpaper to sand the car. This will remove any fuzzies.

52

FINAL SANDING

Once you're completely finished shaping the car, it's time to start sanding the car smooth. Below are various sanding tools that help get the job finished quickly. It can take a while to get all the marks and scratches out of the body. Start with 100-grit paper if your car has very large saw marks to remove. Move on to 150-grit and then finish up with 220-grit paper.

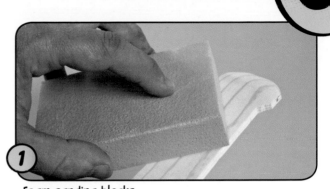

1

Foam sanding blocks.
These blocks are easy for kids to use and they come in 100- and 150-grit sandpaper.

SANDING BLOCKS
* 100 & 150 grit

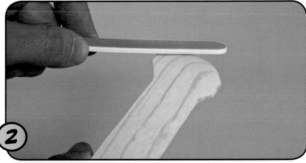

2

Emery Boards.
These sanding sticks are very handy and can fit into tighter spots than the larger sanding blocks. They come in many different sanding grits.

EMERY BOARDS
* 100 & 180 grit
* 280 & 320 grit

SANDPAPER
* 100, 150 & 220 grit

3

Sandpaper.
Sandpaper is the most common sanding tool. Cut full sheets into 4 equal pieces. Take one of those pieces and fold it in half and then in half again. As the sandpaper wears out, unfold and then refold the paper in a different order to expose fresh unused sandpaper.

5

CHAPTER 4
WEIGHTING

Now we need to add weight to get your car up to 5.0 ounces. There are two key points to remember. You want as much weight in the back as possible. But, at the same time, you don't want too much weight back there, causing your car to pop wheelies down the track. You want your car to have a balance point, or center of gravity, in front of the rear axle. See page 18 for more information on setting the balance point.

Read about the different types of weights and then follow the directions to add the weights to your car. Follow the steps for drilling the holes, and then jump to the steps on attaching the weights.

lbs.

Professor Speed here! I've been experimenting with weight and Pinewood Derby cars for years. Follow my simple steps and you'll have the fastest car at the Derby.

TYPES OF WEIGHT

There are many types of metal you can use to add weight to your car. I have seen all types of things used, including coins, washers, and even nuts and bolts. I get asked all the time about what is the best type of weight to use. A lot depends on the type of car you're building. Very thin cars are easier to build with tungsten weights. Tungsten is very dense, so you can fit a lot more weight in a small space than you can with lead. Now, tungsten is available in many useful shapes, making weighting your car even easier. The downsides of tungsten are you can't reshape it and it costs a lot more per ounce than lead weights.

Lead has been the classic weight for Pinewood Derby cars. It's easy to shape and cut, and it's cheap. But it's also less dense than tungsten and toxic. You must be very careful using lead and it must be completely sealed inside the car if you choose to use it.

TUNGSTEN CYLINDERS
* Very dense
* Available in three weights
* Fits into a drilled hole
* Non-toxic

TUNGSTEN SLOTTED DISCS
* Can adjust the weight by adding two tungsten cubes
* Fits into a 1" drilled hole
* Available in two weights
* Non-toxic

LEAD WIRE
* Easy to seal inside your car
* Cheaper than tungsten
* Doesn't require shaping or melting

TUNGSTEN CUBES
* Packs a lot of weight in a tight space
* Easy to adjust your weight
* Can be placed very low in your car
* Non-toxic

TUNGSTEN CANOPIES
* Easy to install
* Adds to the design
* Available in two weights
* Non-toxic

LEAD SPLIT SHOT
* Useful to fine tune center balance
* Can be used in your trim holes
* Available at all fishing shops
* Soft, can be pressed into holes

TUNGSTEN PUTTY
* Can be molded into different spaces
* Useful to fine tune center balance
* Can be used in your trim holes

ADDING WEIGHT

The first step you need to do is weight all the parts of your car. You will need your car body, four wheels and four axles and a digital scale. Set the scale to read ounces. Start by placing all your parts on the scale and then start to add your selected weight. Your target weight is 4.8 ounces. The remaining 0.2 ounces will be added when you paint your car and with the final trim weight.

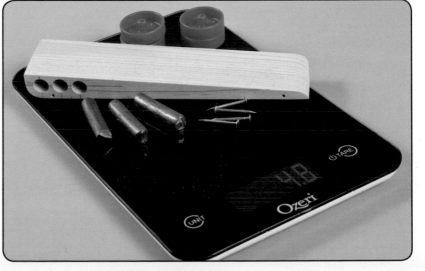

LEAD WIRE

Lead has been used for a very long time to add weight to Pinewood Derby cars. In the past, lead would be melted and poured directly into cars. But now you can purchase lead in ³/₈" rods. This saves you from the dangers of melting and sanding lead. Remember, always use caution when handling lead.

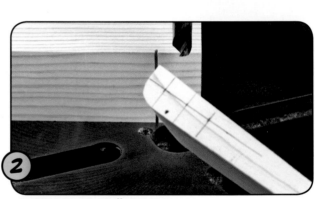

1

Transfer the measurement to the car.
Follow the drawing at right to determine the best location for the lead pieces.

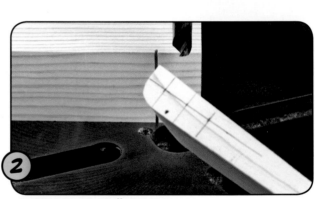

2

Ready to start drilling.
Mount a ²⁵/₆₄" drill bit into your drill press.

3

Set the depth of the drill.
Wrap a piece of tape around a ²⁵/₆₄"drill bit to set the drilling depth to 1¹¹/₁₆".

4

Drill the holes.
Use a second wooden block to help keep your car 90° to the drill table.

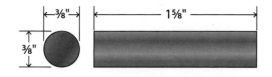

Remember, always use caution when handling lead (see page 14).

Number of Pieces	Weight
1	1.1 oz
2	2.2 oz
3	3.3 oz

5

Clean out the holes.
Remove any wood chips that remain in the holes.

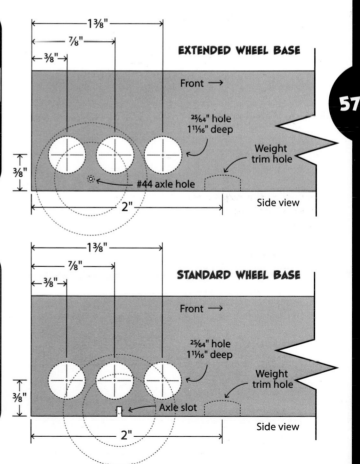

EXTENDED WHEEL BASE

Front →

²⁵⁄₆₄" hole 1¹¹⁄₁₆" deep

Weight trim hole

#44 axle hole

Side view

STANDARD WHEEL BASE

Front →

²⁵⁄₆₄" hole 1¹¹⁄₁₆" deep

Weight trim hole

Axle slot

Side view

6

Test fit the lead pieces.
Dry fit the lead pieces completely into the holes to ensure they don't stick out the side.

TUNGSTEN CYLINDERS

Tungsten is the perfect material to add weight to a pinewood derby car. With a density comparable to gold, it's 1.7 times more dense than lead and 2.7 times as dense as zinc. Because you can't reshape the tungsten pieces, it's sold in many different sizes and shapes.

This type of tungsten is shaped into cylinders and can be inserted into $^{25}/_{64}$" holes in your car. It's available in full, half, and quarter cylinders to allow you to get your weight exactly where you need it. It can be installed in the bottom of the car as shown or you can install it the same way as lead wire on page 56.

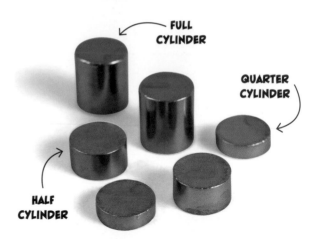

FULL CYLINDER

QUARTER CYLINDER

HALF CYLINDER

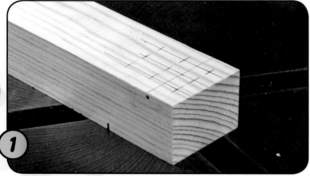

1

Transfer the measurements to the car.
Follow the drawing on page 59 to determine the best location for the tungsten cylinders.

2

Set the depth of the drill.
Wrap a piece of tape around a $^{25}/_{64}$" drill bit to set the drilling depth to $^{3}/_{8}$".

3

Drill the holes.
Carefully drill each of the nine holes. Drilling slowly will produce the cleanest holes with very little tear-out around the holes.

4

Clean out the holes.
Remove any wood chips that remain in the holes.

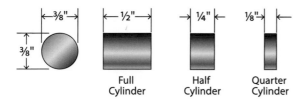

Cylinders Size	Weight
Full Cylinder	.5 oz
Half Cylinder	.25 oz
Quarter Cylinder	.125 oz

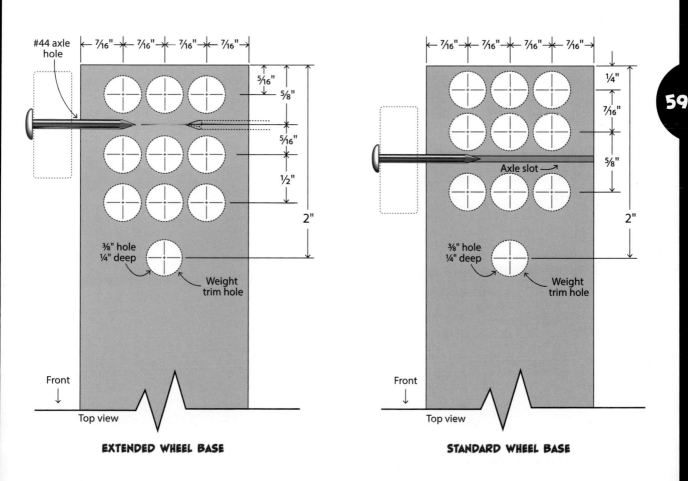

EXTENDED WHEEL BASE

STANDARD WHEEL BASE

59

TUNGSTEN SLOTTED DISC

This type of tungsten can be installed with very little work. It comes in two weights; 2.6 oz and 3.2 oz. Simply drill a 1"-diameter hole in the bottom of your car to the correct depth and drop the weight into the hole. It's that easy! After you get your car painted and you're in the final assembly stages, add a dab of glue into the hole to secure the disc. That way you can easily remove the disc and reuse it next year! If the car is still a little under the weight, you can add two tungsten cubes into the center of the slot between the axle points. That will give you an additional .34 oz of weight. See page 62 for more information on tungsten cubes.

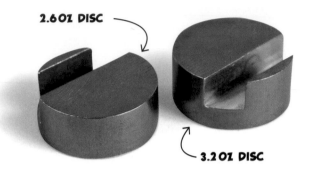

2.6 OZ DISC

3.2 OZ DISC

60

1

Selecting your drill bit.
You have two options to drill the 1"-diameter hole: a forstner bit (left) or a spade bit (right). The forstner bit is the better choice for thinner cars.

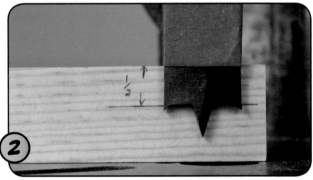

2

Setting the depth for the 3.2 oz disc.
Measure ½" from the flat part of the spade bit and wrap a piece of painter's tape around the bit to set the depth. Some spade bits have long points that can easily go though the top of your car body. If you have this problem, you can fill this hole with wood filler.

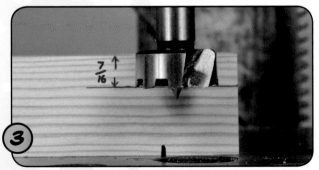

3

Setting the depth for the 2.6 oz disc.
Measure ⁷⁄₁₆" from the flat part of the forstner bit and wrap a piece of painter's tape around the bit to set the depth if necessary. The forstner bit shown was exactly ⁷⁄₁₆" deep.

4

Clean out the hole.
Remove any wood chips that remain in the hole.

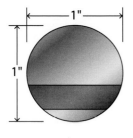

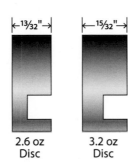

2.6 oz
Disc

3.2 oz
Disc

Disc Weight	Hole Depth
2.6 oz	⁷⁄₁₆"
3.2 oz	½"

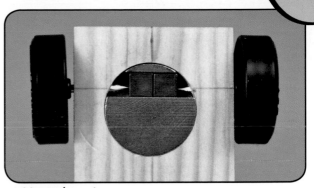

Additional weight.
If you need a little bit more weight you can slide two tungsten cubes into the slot and between the axle points. This will give you an additional .34 oz of weight.

Need more weight?
Add two tungsten cubes between the axle points.

Two cubes = .34 oz

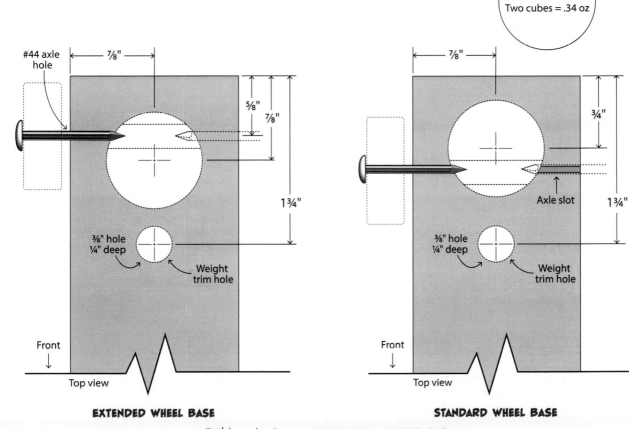

#44 axle hole

⅞"

⅝"

⅞"

1¾"

⅜" hole
¼" deep

Weight trim hole

Front

Top view

EXTENDED WHEEL BASE

⅞"

¾"

Axle slot

1¾"

⅜" hole
¼" deep

Weight trim hole

Front

Top view

STANDARD WHEEL BASE

TUNGSTEN CUBES

If you have a super-thin car and you need a lot of weight, you can't go wrong with tungsten cubes. Because they are square, you can stack them together and create a variety of shapes. Carving out a pocket in the bottom of the car is a bit more difficult than drilling holes, though.

A second option would be to design your car to only be ¼" thick and cut the pocket straight though the car body. Next, cut a thin piece of cardboard from a cereal box and glue it to the top of the car to cover the weight pocket. Then, install the cubes into the pocket and seal the bottom with a second piece of cardboard. Make sure you pack the cubes in tight so they can't move, or add a little glue to stop them from moving around. Many packs will disqualify cars with weights that are loose inside the body.

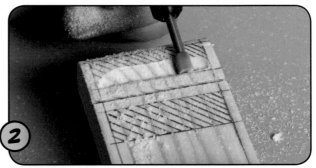

1

Locating the weight pocket.

Lay out the dimension for the pocket on the bottom of your car using the drawings on page 63. The sample shown is using rows of 5 cubes, but you can get 6 cubes across the body of the car. To do this, you will need to get the corners of your pocket square.

2

Carefully remove material.

Using a Dremel and a hi-speed-steel cutter bit, slowly remove material from the center of the pocket.

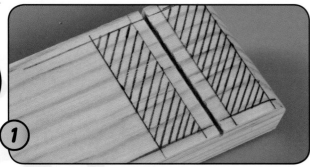

3

Flatten the bottom of the pocket.

Pressing the top of the cutter head into the bottom of the pocket, slowly move the bit back and forth to smooth out the bottom of the pocket.

4

Test fit the cubes.

Install all the cubes into the pocket to make sure everything fits. Make any adjustments necessary.

TIP WHERE TO BUY TUNGSTEN?

Until recently, tungsten weights were only available from online pinewood derby suppliers or well-stocked hobby shops. But, in the past few years, tungsten weights are now sold at local craft stores in the pinewood derby section. They come in plate form (below), cylinders, and putty. If you plan to use the plate style, cut a pocket into the bottom of the car similar to the tungsten cubes on this page.

Number of Cubes	Weight
1	.17 oz
2	.34 oz
3	.51 oz
4	.68 oz
5	.85 oz
6	1.0 oz
7	1.19 oz
8	1.36 oz
9	1.53 oz
10	1.7 oz
11	1.87 oz
12	2.0 oz

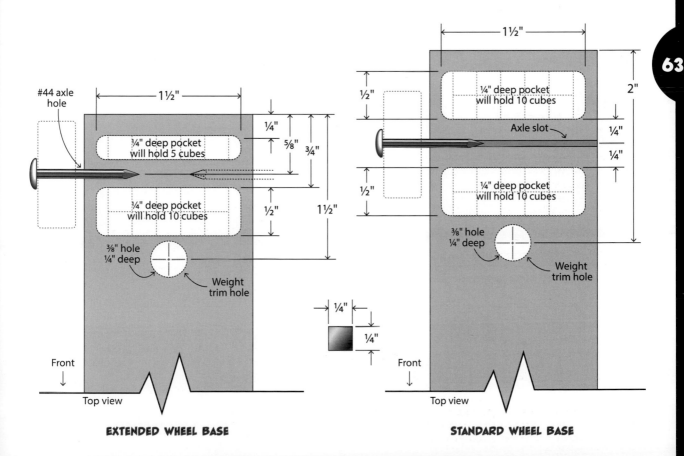

EXTENDED WHEEL BASE

STANDARD WHEEL BASE

TUNGSTEN CANOPIES

The absolute easiest type of tungsten weight to install is a tungsten canopy. And on top of that, they add style to your flat car. They come in two sizes to complement different designs. And they can be removed after the race and used on your car next year!

1

Locating the mounting hole.
Use the drawing on page 65 as your guide to drill the required mounting hole.

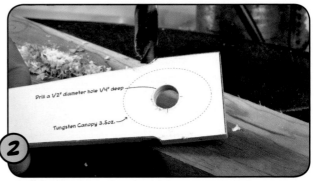

2

Drill bit size.
Make sure you're using the correct drill bit size for your canopy.

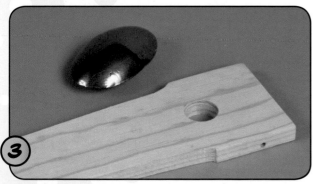

3

Test fit the canopy.
The 2.5 oz canopy uses a ²⁵⁄₆₄" bit and the 3.5 oz canopy uses a ½" drill bit.

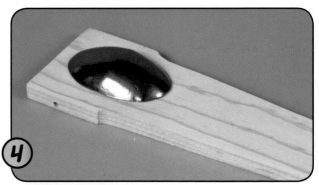

4

Install the canopy.
Firmly press the canopy into the mounting hole. If your canopy is loose, add a little glue to the hole before the final installation.

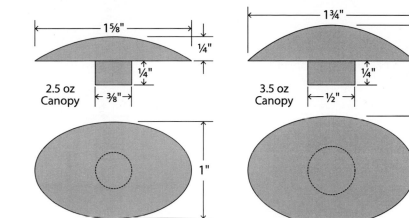

Canopy Weight	Hole Size
2.5 oz	25/64"
3.5 oz	1/2"

65

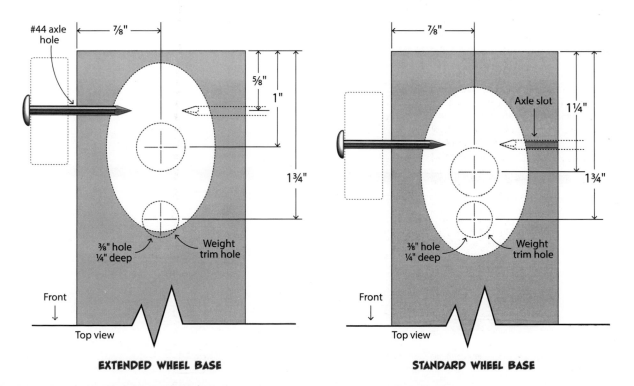

EXTENDED WHEEL BASE

STANDARD WHEEL BASE

WEIGHTING

ATTACHING WEIGHTS

Weights must be completely secured inside the car or it may get disqualified from the race. Many packs prohibit weights moving inside the car body. Remember, if possible, install the weights as low in the car as possible.

USING WOOD PUTTY

1

Using wood filler.
Put an unused axle into the axle hole to protect it from getting filled with wood filler. Add a drop of glue into each hole before you install the weights. Cover the hole with a generous layer of filler.

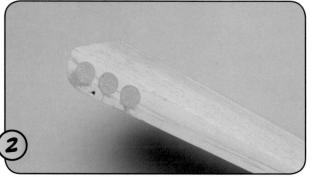

2

Sand the wood filler.
Allow the wood filler to dry overnight and then sand it flush with the car body.

USING EPOXY GLUE

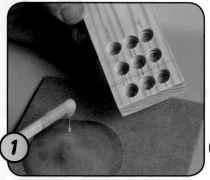

1

Add epoxy into the weight holes.
Using an old pencil or Popsicle stick, coat the sides of the holes with epoxy. Do not over fill the holes, only a light coating on the sides. Then, insert the weights.

2

Making a gluing base.
Cut a small piece of cardboard and cover one side with painter's tape. The epoxy will not stick to the top of the tape.

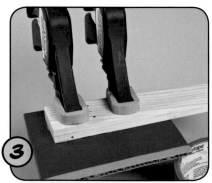

3

Lowering the weights.
Flip the car into the gluing base and clamp them together. Then, tap the car to get the weights to slide to the bottom of the holes. After the epoxy sets up, the bottom of your car will be smooth and the weights will be as low as they can be in the car.

TRIM WEIGHTS

Trim weights are designed to allow weight to be added to the car after it's assembled. They can be used to get a car up to the maximum weight and they can be used to adjust the center of balance. Almost anything could be used as a trim weight. I've seen washers, pennies, or even small screws. Below are just two types of trim weight you can use.

TUNGSTEN PUTTY

1

How much to add.
Use a digital scale to determine how much weight you need to add. See page 127 for more information on final weighting.

2

Pressing in the putty.
Work the putty with your fingers to loosen it up. It will get softer the warmer it gets. Press the putty into the trim holes. The putty will stay in the holes by itself.

SPLIT SHOT

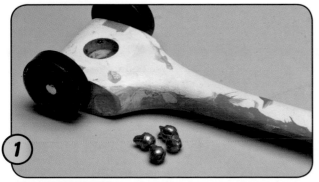

1

How much to add.
Use a digital scale to determine how much weight you need to add. See page 127 for more information on final weighting. If the split shot sticks out below the bottom of the car, use a small hammer to press it into the holes.

2

Gluing in the weight.
If you're adding the split shot at home, you can use white glue to hold it in place. But, if you're adding the weight at the weigh-in of the race, use a few drops of quick-drying super glue to hold the weights in place.

CHAPTER 5
FINISHING

I'm back to show you the coolest part of making a Pinewood Derby car. You get to colorize your car and make it look as wild as you want!

Now that the car is shaped and weighted, the next step is Finishing, or decorating the car. There are a ton of ways to customize your Pinewood Derby car, and many methods are shown here. If you're Feeling lazy, stickers and permanent markers are quick and easy options. However, if you're Feeling more ambitious, you could pick up an airbrush and make the car look really professional and sleek. There are a million and one choices in between. Read through this chapter, get some ideas, and don't be afraid to let your imagination get going! As long as you don't change the shape of the car, the Finishing you apply won't have much of an effect on the car's speed—so have at it.

TYPES OF FINISH

You can use almost any type of marker, paint, sticker, or tape to decorate your car. Use your imagination and see what you have around the house before you spend money on new decorations.

SPRAY PAINT

SCRAPBOOK PAPER

COLORED DUCT TAPE

CLEAR NAIL POLISH

PAINT BRUSHES

BRUSH PAINT

DECALS

PERMANENT MARKERS

FILM COVERING

69

AIR BRUSH

MASKING & TRIM TAPE

BRUSH PAINTING

Acrylic paints are the easiest for young children to use. They are affordable and they come in a wide selection of colors. They also produce very nice results. They are also water based, making cleanup easy.

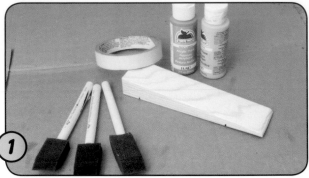

① Prepare your area.
Cover your work surface with newspaper or cardboard. Gather any supplies you will need, such as foam brushes, paint, and tape.

70

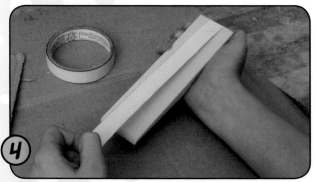

② Prepare to paint.
Cover the area around the axle slots with tape to keep paint from filling the slots. Press the tape firmly in place. Paint around the axle slots will cause friction with the wheels and slow your car.

③ Paint the stripe.
Using a foam brush and acrylic paint, paint the top of the car with the color for the center stripe. Allow the paint to dry for an hour. If desired, use a hair dryer to speed up the drying time.

④ Cover the stripe.
Place a piece of ¾"-wide tape down the center of the block. Firmly press down the tape. This will keep the second color off the center area, giving you a clean striped effect.

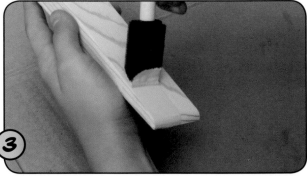

⑤ Paint the second color.
Paint the second color over the entire car. Place the car over the handles of two foam brushes to raise the car so you can paint down the sides. This keeps the car from sticking to the work surface. Allow the paint to dry.

Second coat if necessary.
Apply a second coat of paint, if the first color can still be seen through the first coat.

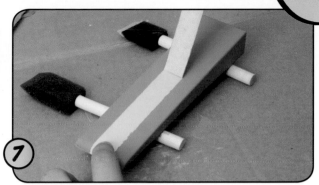

Remove the tape.
Carefully remove the tape from the center stripe.

Allow the paint to dry.
Make sure the paint is completely dry before moving on to the next step.

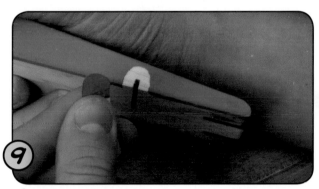

Remove remaining tape.
Remove the tape from the axle areas.

71

Add pin stripes.
Apply ⅛" pin-striping tape where the colors join to cover any areas where the paint ran under the tape.

ACRYLIC
PAINTS

SPRAY PAINTING

Spray painting is a more advanced technique, but it produces a finish comparable to an automotive finish. The system shown is a two-step process, with a base color and a shiny clear coat. With a little practice, children can also master this technique.

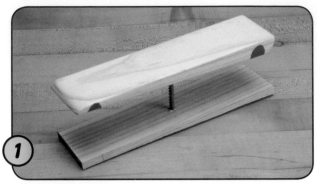

(1)

Prepare the car.
Tape over the axle holes or slots with painter's tape. Construct a paint stand to hold your car that allows the top and bottom to be painted at the same time. This is a simple stand made from a scrap of wood and a 2" screw.

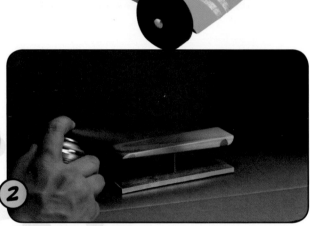

(2)

Apply the accent color.
Begin by spraying a light coat of your accent color. This coat is your sealer and primer. Allow to dry for 30 minutes.

(3)

Sand the first coat.
The car will be rough after the first coat. Sand the entire surface with 220-grit sandpaper. Refold the sandpaper as it becomes covered with removed paint. Spray with a second coat and allow to dry.

(4)

Masking the accent design.
Apply a piece of painter's tape to a sheet of waxed paper. Trace the desired design onto the tape. Cut the design out with a pair of scissors.

(5)

Apply the accent design.
Peel off the waxed paper from your design and apply the design to the car.

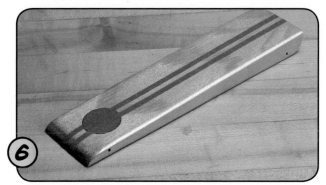

Adding accent stripes.
Cut two ⅛" stripes of painters tape. Press them firmly to the car.

Apply the main color.
Spray the main color in several light coats, instead of one heavy coat.

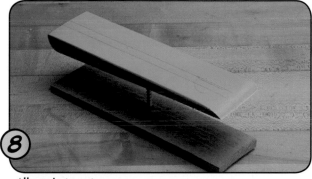

Allow drying time.
Allow the paint to thoroughly dry. Refer to the manufacturer's recommended drying time.

Remove the painters tape.
Remove the tape from all areas except the axle holes or slots.

73

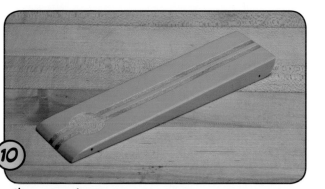

Clear coat the car.
Apply several light coats of clear paint. Allow to dry completely. Remove the remaining painter's tape. See pages 81 and 82 for information on adding decals.

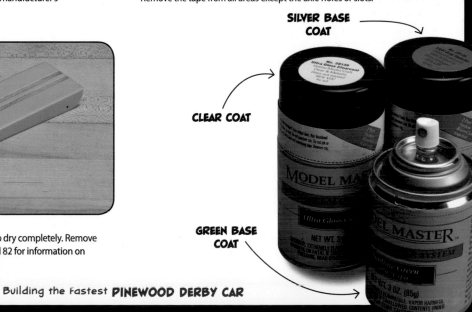

SILVER BASE COAT

CLEAR COAT

GREEN BASE COAT

AIRBRUSH PAINTING

There are several affordable airbrushes on the market that are easy for children to use. This system from Testors allows you to spray directly from the bottles. Airbrushing allows you to achieve painting effects that you cannot do with brushes or spray paints. In this example, we are demonstrating a simple color fading technique. But, you can use your imagination to dream up any possible design.

1

Gather the materials.
Lay a piece of paper or cardboard on your spraying surface to protect it from overspray or spilled paint. In this example, I have already painted the car with a base coat of white.

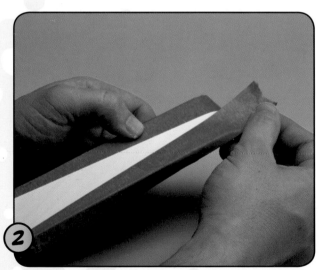

2

Masking your design.
Use painter's tape to create your custom design. Cover the areas that you want to remain the base color. Remember to cover the axle holes or slots with painter's tape.

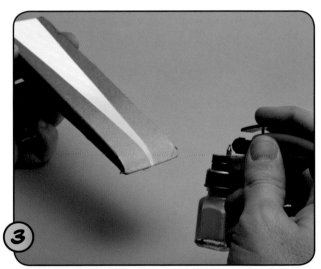

3

Begin to spray yellow.
Begin to spray with the lightest color. Apply several thin coats only to the front of the car.

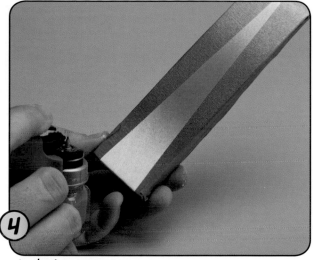

Apply the orange.
If you want to achieve the fade design, hold the car from the back, and lightly spray the middle of the car, fading the orange into the yellow.

Apply the red.
Continuing spraying from the back of the car, fading the red into the orange. Make sure to spray the back end of the car.

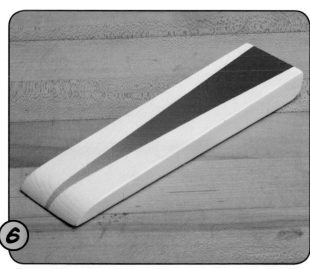

Remove the tape.
Allow the car to thoroughly dry. Carefully remove the painter's tape from all areas. See page 82 for information on adding pin stripes to this design.

BASIC AIRBRUSH SET

WRAPPING WITH PAPER

Paper is a great way to wrap your car in a colorful pattern. Try wrapping paper, newspaper, scrapbook paper, comic book pages, or whatever else you can find! The instructions for all of them will be the same as you see here.

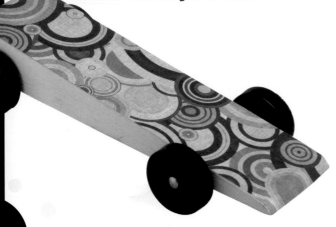

Gather the materials.
Prepare your car by applying two coats of paint, allowing it to dry, and then sanding the top surface smooth. Get some scrapbook paper, glue, and a foam brush.

76

Mark up the paper.
Decide what section of the paper you want to put on your car. Put the car down and trace along both sides. Move the car and use a ruler to extend the lines the whole way to the edge of the paper.

Tape the strip.
Use scissors to cut along the lines you traced. Place the car on the paper and cut off any excess paper. Use a piece of tape to keep the paper aligned on the car.

4

Apply glue.
Put some glue on a scrap of wood or paper. Use a foam brush to apply glue to the top surface of the car.

5

Affix the paper.
Flip the car over so the top is down. Stretch the paper firmly and press the car down to the paper. Glue around the edge and fix the paper to the bottom.

6

Mix the top layer of thinned glue.
Mix 3 parts glue and 1 part water.

7

Apply the thinned glue.
Use a foam brush to apply the thinned glue to the bottom flaps, sides, and top. Wait for it to dry and apply a second coat.

PERMANENT MARKERS

Permanent markers are a quick way to make a custom finish on your car. You can choose from any of the colors in the rainbow. Make sure you don't get any permanent marker on anything besides your car though! It is **permanent.**

1

Pencil in the design.
Use a pencil to draw on what you want. Then decide what colors to use and start filling in the areas with the lightest colors.

2

Blending the colors.
Add the next color. Before the darker color dries, rub it into the lighter color. Continue to add and blend darker colors.

3

Outline the areas.
Use a dark color to outline the light areas. Don't hold the marker in one place too long, or the ink will bleed past the line where you want it.

4

Add the other colors.
Color in all the other areas that are left. Fill in large areas by drawing with the wood grain. This will keep all the lines going the same way and keep your finish from looking scribbled.

PERMANENT MARKERS

DUCT TAPE

Duct tape is an easy way to apply finish to your car without the mess of paints or markers. There is a wide selection of colors and patterns available at craft stores. From skull and crossbones to colorful tie-dye, you're only limited by your imagination.

Wrap the bottom of the car.

Starting on the bottom of the car, apply the tape to the bottom and then wrap it up the sides and back. Cut some of the tape from the corners before you wrap the tape to avoid thick build-up of tape along the corners.

Cover the top of the car.

Use scissors to trim the tape even with the top of the car. Apply a piece of tape to the top of the car. Use scissors to trim this tape to the edges of the car.

Add decorations.

Apply any decorations you would like. In the example, I've trimmed a strip of checkerboard tape and applied it down the center of the car.

Trim the areas around the wheels.

Use a hobby knife to remove the tape around the axle holes or axle shots.

DUCT TAPE ROLLS

DUCT TAPE SHEETS

FILM COVERING

Iron-on film covering is sold to cover the airframes of radio-controlled airplanes. It makes a very lightweight and smooth finish. It is available in hobby shops in a wide range of colors and finishes. You can get solid color, transparent, neon, metallic, and pearls.

1

Gather your materials.
In this example, I have chosen a transparent red to highlight the ribbed structure of this car design. You will need a standard home iron or a sealing iron, like shown above, and a hobby knife.

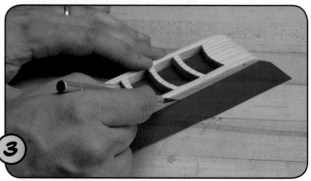

2

Sealing the edges.
Cut a piece of the film larger then the bottom of the car. Start by ironing the edges along the bottom of the car. Start in the middle and work your way out to the edges. Once all the edges are sealed, iron over the bottom of the car to stretch the film tight. You can use a pin to remove air trapped under the film.

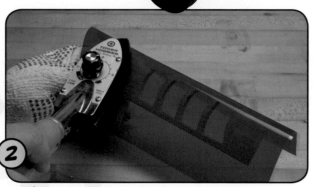

3

Trim the edges.
Use a hobby knife to trim the film to the edges of the car.

4

Covering the top of the car.
Repeat the same process in Step 2 and cover the top, but this time iron the film down over the edges of the car. Trim the edges of the film even with the bottom of the car.

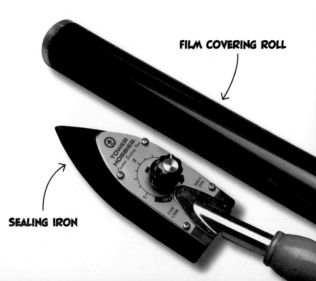

FILM COVERING ROLL

SEALING IRON

FINAL TOUCHES

WATER SLIDE DECALS

Water slide decals are the type of decals you will find in plastic model kits. They are my favorite type of decals because they have a superior finish to all other decals. Water slide decals can be placed on curved surfaces without the problem of wrinkles you will find with peel-and-stick decals. It's a good idea to seal the decals under a protective layer of clear coat paint. Remember, always test any type of sealing paint on a test surface with a decal before you spray your car. You don't won't to ruin the finish of your car when you're so close to being done building it!

Cut out the decal.
Use a sharp pair of scissors to loosely cut out the decal from the full sheet of decals. There is no need to trim to the edges of the decal.

Soak the decal in water.
Let the decal soak in a small bowl of lukewarm water for 30 seconds. Try to move the decal on its backing paper to see if the decal to ready. If the decal slides freely on if backing paper, it's ready to be applied to the car.

Position the decal.
Don't remove the decal from the backing paper. Slide the wet decal partially off its backing paper. Carefully place the decal close to its final location. Slide it the rest of the way off the backing paper.

Adjust the location.
You can easily move the decal into your desired location. Once you are happy with the location of the decal, carefully press a paper towel on top of it to remove any remaining water. Once the decal is dry, it's a good idea to seal it under a protective clear coat of paint.

81

FINAL TOUCHES

DRY TRANSFER

Dry transfer or rub-on decals are applied by pressing them on to the surface of your car. My favorite types of dry transfer decals are sheets of letters. That way you can add custom names to your car. You can find these types of sheets at craft stores. Make sure to leave the backing sheet attached wherever your hand is resting. Any pressure can accidently transfer parts of other letters.

1

Remove the backing sheet.
Slide the backing sheet to reveal the letter your planning to transfer. Use a Popsicle stick and rub across the surface to press the decal onto the surface up your car.

2

Peeling off the carrying sheet.
Carefully peel the carrier sheet off, starting at the corner of the letter. Be careful not to lift the letter off the surface of the car.

3

The Final decal.
Make sure the spacing between the letters is the same and the letters all rest on the same base line.

STRIPING TAPE

Striping tape is a great way to add that final touch to make your car really stand out. It's also great at hiding any areas on your car that may have a flaw in the paint job, like paint that ran under a painter's tape edge.

1

Select your striping tape.
You can find striping tape at hobby shops or auto parts stores. Some types of striping tapes come with a wide and a narrow tape on the same roll.

2

Applying the tape.
Cut a piece of tape longer than you need for your car. Remove the backing and align one end of the tape where you want the stripe to start. Slowly lower the tape the rest of the way onto your car.

3

Press down the tape.
After you apply all the tape, go over all the stripes and firmly press them onto the surface of the car.

HARDENING THE AREA AROUND THE AXLE HOLES

The theme throughout this book is minimizing friction areas. The area of the body where the wheel hub rubs against the body is one such area. You can only get wood so smooth by just sanding it. Wood is very soft, porous and is made up of many rough fibers. You must apply finish onto the wood that will soak into the fibers and harden them. This will allow the wood to be sanded to a very smooth surface. Clear fingernail polish is the perfect finish. It's designed to produce a very hard and durable surface.

1 You will need a bottle of clear nail polish, 220-,400-,600-, 1000-grit sandpaper and your unpainted car body.

2 Start by sanding the areas around the axle holes with 220-grit sandpaper.

3 Brush on two coats of clear nail polish around the axle holes. I like to start the coat ½" before and after the hole. Allow the polish to thoroughly dry.

4 Find a flat object that you can use as a sanding block.

5 Wrap the 400-grit sandpaper around the sanding stick.

6 Sand the nail polish until it's smooth. Repeat on all the axle holes. Do not wet the sandpaper; use it dry.

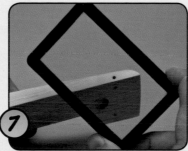

7 Use a magnifying glass to inspect your work. If you don't see any bumps or ridges, continue to the 600-grit sandpaper and repeat Step 6.

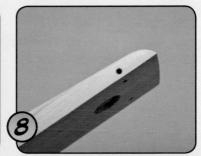

8 Repeat the process for the 1000-grit sandpaper. When you're done, the surface around your axle holes will be amazingly smooth.

FINISHING IDEAS

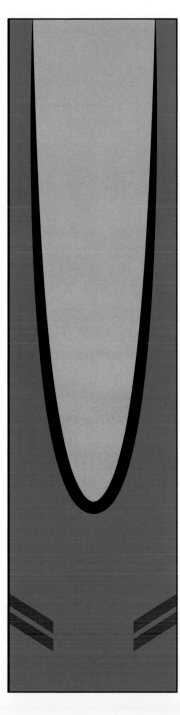

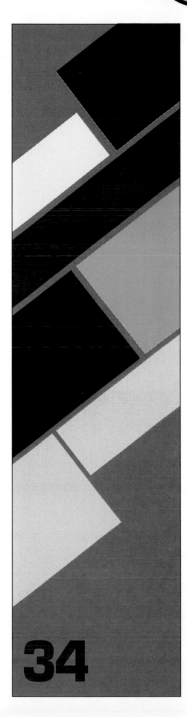

FINISHING IDEAS

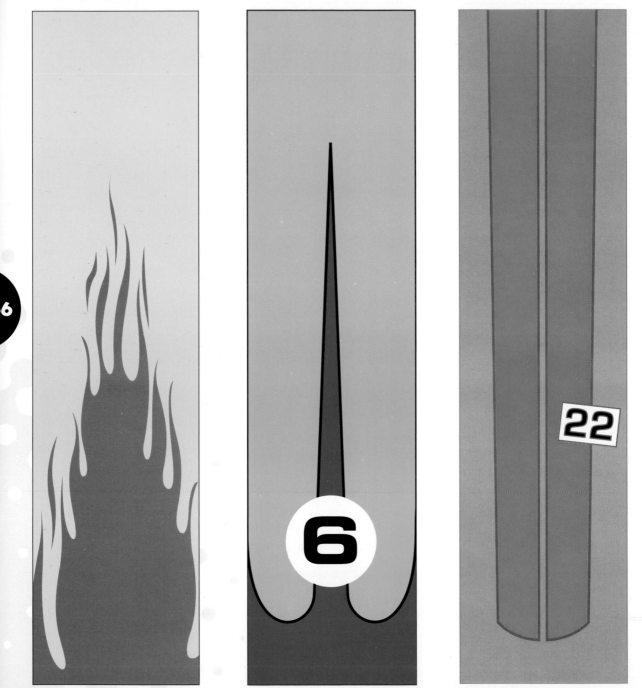

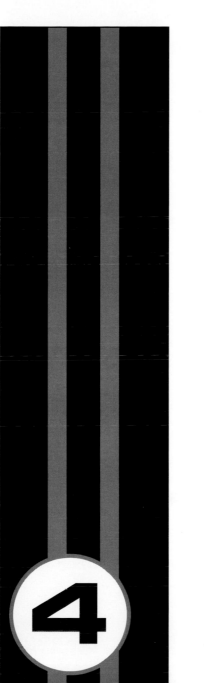

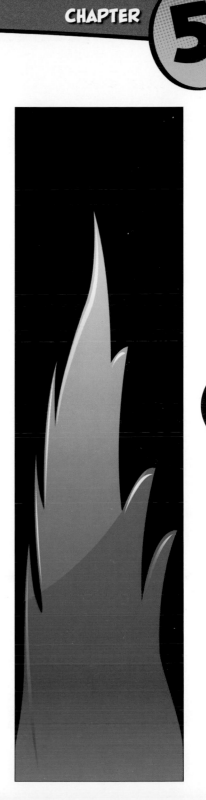

AXLE PREP

I'm back to teach you about preparing the axles on your car. This might sound boring, but prepping the axles properly will make your car very fast!

In this section, I will introduce the two steps in axle preparation that you must complete to have a competitive car—removing burrs and polishing your axles. All Official Pinewood Derby axles have burrs, which must be sanded off to decrease friction. Polishing your axles will also cut down on friction. As the car moves down the track, the wheels turn and rub on the axle shaft continually. It is essential that the axle surface be as smooth and as shiny as possible. You need to polish, polish, polish those axles until they shine like mirrors! All competitive cars have polished axles, but some are polished better than others. The method I'm demonstrating here has been used for several years and will give your axles a better polish than most other methods.

Keep in mind that this is a great place for your child to do a major portion of the work—just be sure to teach principles as you work. Make sure they understand why each step in the building process is being performed. You might even have a contest to see who can make their axles shine the brightest! Remember to make the building process fun.

AXLE PREP TOOLS

There are many axle prep tools you can use to get your car's axles super-polished and friction-free. The tools pictured here will help you on your way to perfect axles.

CORDLESS DRILL

MAGNIFYING GLASS

POLISHING PAPER

TRIANGULAR FILE

FLAT FILE

PERMANENT MARKER

WATER DISH

WET/DRY SANDPAPER

REMOVING THE BURRS

All Official BSA axles, when they first come out of the box, have a set of small burrs located underneath the head of the axle. Whenever the wheel and the axle head touch, these little burrs create a large amount of friction. The burrs are almost like mini brakes, so they must be removed. The underside of the axle head must be polished smooth as well. Remember that friction is the enemy of speed, and these little burrs are a major source of friction.

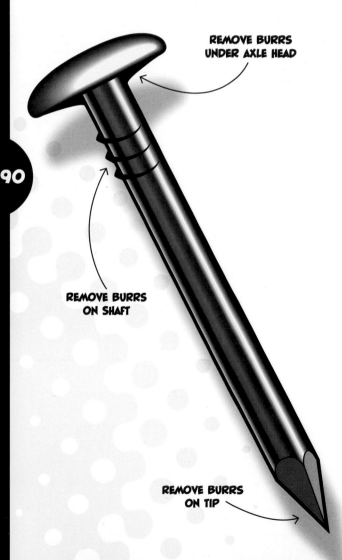

REMOVE BURRS
UNDER AXLE HEAD

REMOVE BURRS
ON SHAFT

REMOVE BURRS
ON TIP

Raw axles.
Notice the burrs that are present on all official BSA axles, which come in the box with the rest of the materials. We will be removing them using an electric drill and a small triangular file.

Set up your workspace.
Most cordless drills will stand upright on their battery pack. An adult can hold the drill steady and control the drill speed.

Insert an axle into the drill.
Leave about half an inch exposed. Be sure that the axle is tightly secured in the drill. For this process we will only be using the drill to hold the axle steady. You will not be spinning the axle.

4

File away burrs.
With the drill not spinning, use a triangular file to remove the burrs. Put only light pressure on the file so you do not damage the axle in the process of removing the burrs.

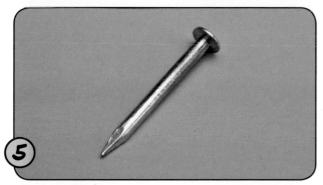

5

De-burred axles.
Make sure to remove the burrs under the head of the axle. Any burrs on the tip of the axle should be filed away also, so as not to enlarge the holes or slots in the block. The finished axles should look like the one shown here.

TIP FIND THE BEST AXLES

There's no such thing as a straight axle that comes directly out of the box, but some are much straighter than others. This concept is very important to understand. If you use axles that are curved or bent, your wheels will wobble as they go down the track. Bent axles will also affect the alignment of your wheels. Simply put, Bent Axles = Less Speed.

The difference between a good axle and a bad axle is not normally visible to the naked eye. Using a drill press or a handheld drill, however, we can find the best axles of the bunch.

1

In order to find a good set of straight axles, you will need to start with about 20 raw axles. To get additional axles, you'll need to buy extra axle/wheel sets.

2

Take each axle and put a small mark on it about ½" down from the sharp, pointed end. Then, insert the axle into a cordless power drill or a drill press to the previously marked location.

3

Turn the drill on medium speed and observe the spinning axle. Bent axles, like the one shown here, will wobble as they turn in the drill. All axles will wobble to some degree. The idea here is to pick the four axles that appear to wobble the least amount.

TAPER THE AXLE HEAD

As the axle head and the wheel rub against each other, they create friction, which slows your car down. You can minimize this friction by tapering the head of the axle with an electric drill and a small triangular file. This makes the area of the axle head that touches the wheel much smaller.

5° taper

TAPER THE UNDERSIDE OF THE AXLE

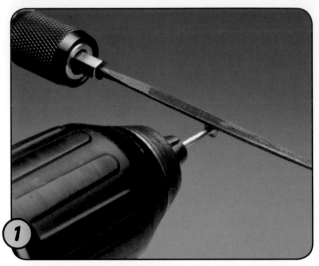

1

Start with a triangular file.
Using a smooth-tooth file, gently file the axle head to an angle of about 5°.

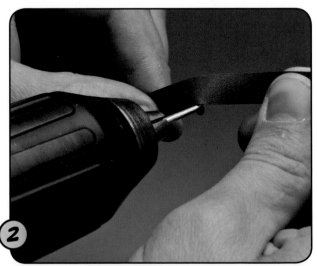

2

Remove the file scratches.
Select a sheet of 400-grit sandpaper and cut a small strip about ¼" wide and 4" long. Dip the strip of sandpaper into the small dish of water, and then apply it to the axle to polish the taper that you just filed. Then, continue with the Polishing the Axles instructions found on page 94.

THE DERBY WORX PRO-AXLE PRESS

The Pro-Axle Press will improve the speed of your Pinewood Derby car by performing three critical procedures on your axles:

Axle Straightening - Ensures accurate wheel tracking by creating absolutely straight axles.

Axle Rounding - Ensures accurate wheel rotation by creating rounder axle shafts.

Head Squaring - Ensures proper wheel rotation by squaring the axle head to the axle shaft.

1 Insert an axle into the chuck of a drill. Use a file to remove the burr under the nail head and any burrs on the axle shaft.

2 Make a mark anywhere on the head of the axle.

3 Fully insert the axle, point first, into the axle press. Rotate the axle head so that the mark is located at the top (the 12 o'clock position), and close the press.

4 Place the press on a solid surface, hold it in place, and strike the top of the press four to six times with a hammer. Don't strike too hard; medium strikes are fine.

5 Open the press and repeat Steps 3 and 4 with the mark at the 4 o'clock position.

93

6 Open the press and repeat Steps 3 and 4 with the mark at the 8 o'clock position.

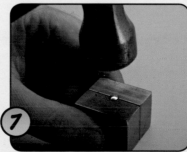

7 After the last strike at the 8 o'clock position, lay the press on its back (axle head upward) and strike the axle head two to four times to ensure that the axle head is square to the axle shaft.

8 Repeat the process for the other three axles, and then polish the axles to the desired finish.

POLISHING THE AXLES

A great deal of friction is created when the wheel rubs against the axle while it is turning. To reduce this friction, make the surface of the axle as smooth as it can be. Believe it or not, the outcome of a race may well depend upon who does the best job polishing their axles.

You can purchase sandpaper kits on the Internet from websites that specialize in Pinewood Derby supplies. The best kits will include 400-, 600-, 1000-, 1500-, 2000-, 2500-, and 3000-grit sandpaper, as well as 2 and 1 micron aluminum oxide polishing paper.

1

Gather the materials.
Have a number of different grits of wet/dry sandpaper on hand.

2

Polishing strips.
Cut one small strip about ¼" wide and 4" long of each of the sandpaper grits and micron paper. Use a marker and write the grit number on the back of the strips.

3

Wet the 400-grit sandpaper strip.
Select a sheet of 400-grit sandpaper to start. Dip the strip into a small dish of water.

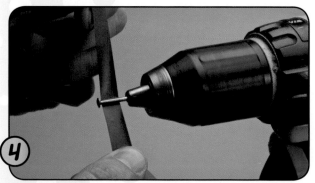

4

Sand the axle.
Turn the drill on medium to high speed and then apply sandpaper to the axle. Be sure to sand the entire axle, including the inside surface of the head. This step should take about 15 seconds. Warning: excessive polishing will reduce the diameter of the axle shaft.

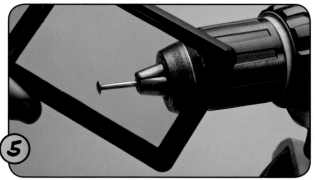

5

Check your progress.
Turn off the drill. Look at the axle with a good magnifying glass. Are there any deep scratches left? If so, then turn the drill back on and polish some more! Do not move to the next step until all of the deep scratches have been removed.

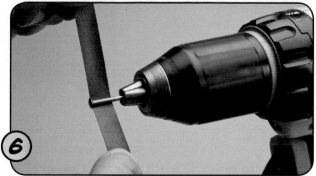

(6)

Repeat with 600-grit sandpaper.
Repeat Steps 3 to 5 using a strip of 600-grit sandpaper. Look at the axle with a magnifying glass after each step to be sure the axle shaft is as smooth as it can be.

(7)

Continue to the next grits.
Repeat Steps 3 to 5 several more times using 1000-, 1200-, 1500-, 2000-, 2500-, and 3000-grit sandpaper.

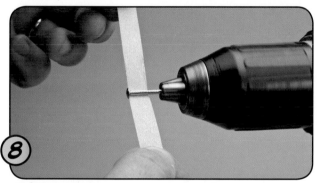

(8)

Polishing paper.
You can achieve an even finer surface by continuing to polish your axles with 1 and 2 micron aluminum oxide polishing paper. Apply the polishing paper to the axle the same as sandpaper but do not use water. Start with the 2 micron paper and then switch to the 1 micron paper.

(9)

Finished axle.
When you've finished sanding, your axles should look like this.

TIP USING A CALLIPER

With a calliper you can measure parts of your pinewood car down to the thousands of an inch. It's very useful to measure the diameter of your axles to help you select the roundest axles. You can use it throughout the polishing process to make sure your not removing too much material from the axles. It can also be used the check the outside diameter of the wheels to identify any wheels that are out of round.

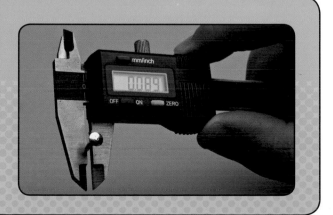

MAKING GROOVED AXLES

Reducing the contact surface between the wheel and the axle will improve the performance of your car. We will reduce the contact surface area by cutting a groove in the axle. The part of the axle where the groove is cut never touches the wheel. This feature significantly improves the performance, especially when using liquid lubricants, with benefits when using dry lubricants as well.

This little speed tip also has a hidden advantage. The groove you cut in the axle becomes a secret trough where graphite gets stored. Later on during the race, some of that graphite will work its way out of the trough and be used to lubricate the inside of your wheels.

This speed tip must be accomplished with a drill press.

FRICTION-REDUCING GROOVE

CHECK YOUR RULES!

Check your local rules. If one of the speed tips discussed in this book is not allowed in your Derby, don't use it. If you want to use a particular speed tip but you aren't sure whether it's legal, clear it with your local race organizer before you start building your car. Be honest—it's the Scouting way!

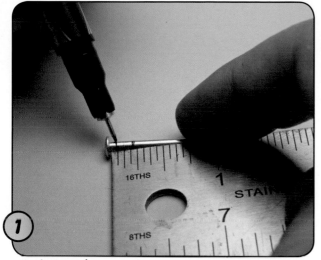

1
Mark the axles.
Place a mark on the axle ¹⁄₁₆" from the head. Place a second mark at ³⁄₁₆".

2
Clamp the axle in your drill.
If you're using a drill press, line up the drill press table with the marks you made on the axle. Use the file to check that everything is aligned.

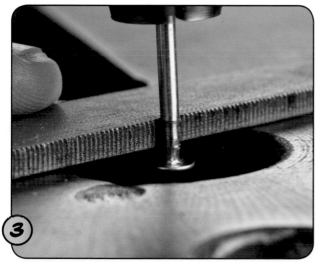

3
Using the flat file.
Gently cut a groove in the axle to a depth less than ¹⁄₁₆". Don't cut the groove too deep; it will weaken the axle.

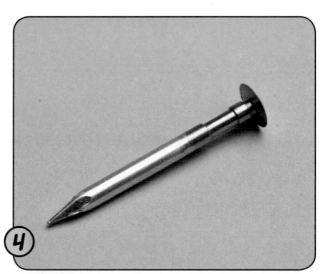

4
Final axle.
Once you have finished polishing the axle according to the method on page 94, the final product should look like the one shown here.

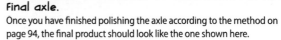

WHEEL PREP

Having the proper wheels will also improve the speed of your car. Follow these tips to increase your speed!

The wheels of a Pinewood Derby car also can determine the speed of the car. They are the only things touching the race track, and so the less friction you can get between the wheel surface and the track surface, the better for your car's speed. The inside bore of your wheels also need to be silky smooth. Read on to unlock the secrets of super-fast wheels.

WHEEL PREP TOOLS

To get your car's wheels as fast as they can be, you'll need a few tools, shown here.

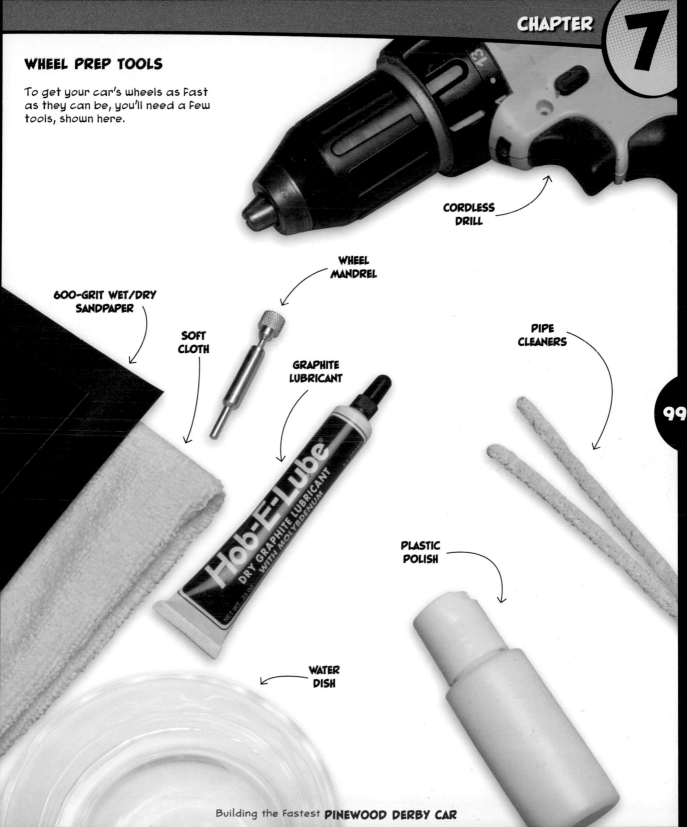

CORDLESS
DRILL

WHEEL
MANDREL

600-GRIT WET/DRY
SANDPAPER

SOFT
CLOTH

GRAPHITE
LUBRICANT

PIPE
CLEANERS

PLASTIC
POLISH

WATER
DISH

99

WHEEL PREP

SELECTING THE BEST WHEELS

Round wheels will help your car track more smoothly. I recommend that you purchase a few extra kits or wheel sets to have a larger selection of wheels to choose from. Building this concentricity gauge will help you quickly and easily check for bad, out-of-round wheels. It's easy to make and costs less than $15.

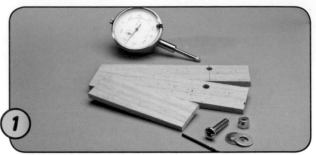

(1)

Gather the materials.

Cut the large paint stirrer into 3 pieces: 4¼" (x 1), 6½" (x 2). Clamp the two long pieces together. Drill (through both pieces) a ¹⁷/₆₄" diameter hole located 1¹¹/₃₂" from the long edge and 1¾" from the short end (see drawing on page 101).

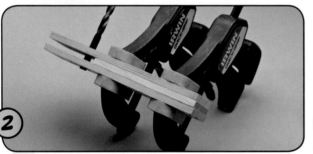

100 (2)

Gluing the parts together.

Spread a very thin layer of wood glue on both sides of the short piece and sandwich it between the two drilled pieces, keeping the top edges and long edges aligned. Slide the shank end of the ¹⁷/₆₄" bit through the drilled holes to keep the longer pieces aligned. Tightly clamp the sandwiched pieces together. Allow the glue to dry before removing the clamps.

(3)

Attaching the gauge.

Remove the clamps. Trim the end with the slot at a 45 degree angle and then round the other end. Sand all the surfaces. Make sure the top edge is flat and square against a flat (preferably machined) surface. Mount the dial indicator to the hole using the bolt, washers, and locknut.

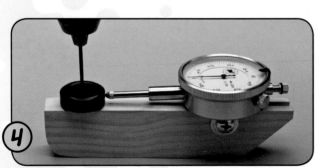

(4)

Adding the testing pin.

Position a spare wheel onto the #41 drill bit. Center the drill bit on the middle wood piece and move the bit toward the dial indicator arm, compressing the dial indicator arm about 40%. When the dial points to the 6 o'clock position, bear down on the drill bit to make a mark on the wood. Drill a #41 hole at the marked location, deep enough to completely cover the fluting of the drill bit. (Use a squared drill press and a fence for this step, if available.) Insert a #41 drill bit into the hole.

TIP USING PIN GAUGES

Pin gauges (also known as plug gauges) are precisely machined rods that measure the width of a hole (the largest gauge that snugly fits determines the diameter). You can use pin gauges to check that your wheels have nearly the same bore size. You can also check the bore as you polish to make sure you don't remove too much plastic. You'll probably just need sizes from 0.0960" to 0.0980".

USING THE GAUGE

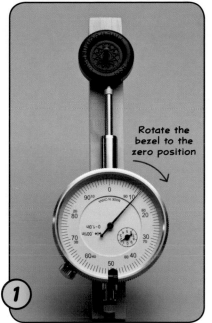

Rotate the
bezel to the
zero position

1

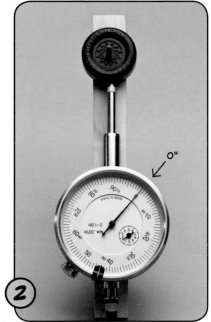

0"

2

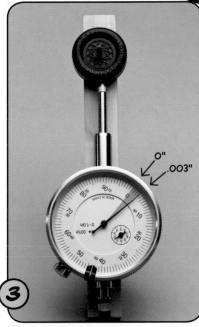

0"

.003"

3

Using the gauge.
Carefully slide a wheel onto the shaft of the #41 drill bit. Rotate the wheel slowly while watching the gauge needle. Stop the wheel at the lowest reading.

"Zero" the gauge.
Rotate the bezel of the gauge so the "0" of the gauge lines up with the needle.

Record your readings.
Rotate the wheel and watch the needle for the highest reading. In the sample above, the highest reading is .003". This wheel is out-of-round by .003". Measure the runout of all wheels and use the four wheels with the lowest readings. Put the worst wheel of the four as the raised front wheel and put the best wheel as the opposite (lowered) front wheel.

Material List

1 – Dial indicator with a ¼"-wide lug on the back (Harbor Freight indicators have this width)

1 – ¼-20 bolt x 1¼" (or machine screw)

1 – ¼" lock nut

2 – ¼" flat washers

1 – #41 drill bit (³⁄₃₂" drill bit will work but the gauge will be less accurate)

1 – ¼"- thick large 5-gal paint stirrer (free from home centers)

Thanks to FatSebastian
From www.derbytalk.com
for this great tool tip.

← 4¼" →

Cut 1

← 6½" → ← 1¾" →

Cut 2

¹¹⁄₃₂"

¹⁷⁄₆₄" hole

Trim corner at 45° angle

Round corner

THE DERBY WORX PRO-WHEEL SHAVER XT

The Pro-Wheel Shaver XT is designed to create round and true wheels by removing tread material from the wheel surface and the wheel edge. This tool is designed to work on hard plastic wheels such as those offered by Boy Scouts of America. It is not intended for wheels made of a relatively soft plastic, such as those offered by Awana.

After all the wheels are trued, follow the steps on page 100 to polish the wheel surfaces and the steps on page 102 to polish the inside rims.

1 To use the Pro-Wheel Shaver XT you must also have a Pro-Hub Tool.

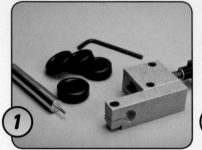

2 Test fit each wheel on the Pro-Hub Tool. Follow the instructions with the Pro-Hub Tool to ream any undersized wheel bores.

3 Slide the Pro-Wheel Shaver XT onto the Pro-Hub Tool, until 1³⁄₁₆" of the Pro-Hub Tool is exposed. Use a ⁵⁄₃₂" hex key to firmly tighten them together.

4 Turn the screw holding the cutting blade, and move the blade towards the Pro-Hub Tool as far as possible. Mount a wheel with the inside wheel hub facing the Pro-Hub Tool.

5 While pressing the wheel against the blade, rotate the wheel five complete revolutions counterclockwise. Remove the wheel and repeat for the remaining wheels.

6 Readjust the Pro-Hub Tool until ⅝" of it is exposed. Then, turn the knob and move the cutting blade into the body of the Pro-Wheel Shaver XT. Mount a wheel with the inside wheel hub facing the Pro-Hub Tool.

7 Rotate the wheel and close the blade to identify the highest spot on the wheel. Rotate the wheel ⅛ to ¼ of a turn and move the blade against the wheel. Press the blade against the wheel; do not press the wheel against the blade.

8 Turn the wheel counterclockwise and make five complete wheel rotations. Slightly loosen the screw connecting the Pro-Wheel Shaver XT to the Pro-Hub Tool. Pull the wheel off and slide the next wheel onto the Pro-Hub.

POLISHING THE INSIDE RIM

The inside of the wheel will rub against the center guide rail of the Pinewood Derby track. Be sure to polish this edge to a very smooth surface to minimize the friction from this contact.

Wheel Mandrel

1

Gather the materials.
You will need a water dish, wheel mandrel, 400-, 600-, and 1000-grit wet/dry sandpaper.

2

Polishing strips.
Cut one strip about ¾" wide and 2" long of each of the sandpaper grits. Use a marker and write the grit number on the back of the strips. Fold the strips in half with the grid facing out.

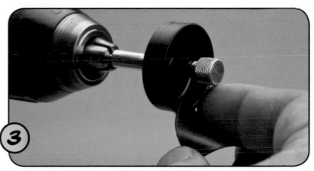

3

Wet the 400-grit sandpaper strip.
Select a sheet of 400-grit sandpaper to start. Dip the strip into a small dish of water. Gently sand the inside wheel rim. Repeat using 600- and then 1000-grit sandpaper.

CHECK YOUR RULES!

Light Weight Speed Wheels.
Machined wheels are available from online Pinewood Derby retailers. The wheels are machined perfectly round and the wheel surfaces are completely flat. In many cases, the wheels have plastic removed form the inside of the wheels. Cars with lighter wheels will start rolling faster at the starting line. Check you local Derby rules before you purchase modified wheels!

Inertia Lite Wheel
1.6 grams

Standard Wheel
2.7 grams

Ultra Lite Wheel
1.0 gram

4

Polish the wheel hub.
Remove the wheel from the wheel mandrel, and lightly sand the wheel hub with 400-grit sandpaper, then repeat with 600- and 1000-grit sandpaper.

WHEEL PREP

POLISHING THE WHEEL BORE

Wheel-to-axle contact is the biggest source of friction on your car. You spent a long time polishing the axles to a mirror finish; now you need to polish the inside of the wheel bore. The best technique I've ever used is to polish the wheel bore with a soft pipe cleaner and plastic polish. You can purchase plastic polish at automotive parts stores or from online Pinewood Derby supply Web sites. You must use soft pipe cleaners designed to clean tobacco pipes. Craft pipe cleaners sold at craft stores will scratch the wheel bore.

Trim the pipe cleaner.
Cut a piece of pipe cleaner about 2.5" long.

Mount the pipe cleaner.
Insert ½" of the pipe cleaner into a cordless drill and tighten the chuck.

Slid on a wheel.
Carefully slide a wheel onto the pipe cleaner.

Apply the plastic polish.
Apply a bead off polish onto the pipe cleaner.

Spread the polish.
Using your finger, spread the polish into the pipe cleaner.

Start polishing.
Hold the wheel in one hand and turn on the drill to a medium speed. Move the wheel back and forth for 30 seconds. Turn off the drill and remove the wheel. Repeat Steps 3 to 6 for the remaining wheels.

Cleaning the wheel bore.
You will need a clean piece of pipe cleaner and a dish of warm water. Soak the wheels in the dish for a few minutes. Wet the pipe cleaner and insert it into the wheel bore. Move the pipe cleaner back and forth to remove any remaining plastic polish. Repeat for the remaining wheels.

Drying the wheel bore.
Insert a clean dry pipe cleaner to dry the wheel bore.

Inspect the results.
Use a magnifying glass to inspect the wheel bore. If you see any imperfection in the wheel bore, repeat the polishing steps.

THE DERBY WORX PRO-BORE POLISHER

If your drill chuck can't clamp down tight enough the hold the pipe cleaner from spinning, you can use this handy tool. The shaft on the end of this tool is much larger than the end of a pipe cleaner so your drill will easily clamp tight.

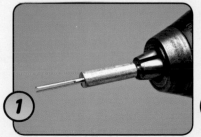

Insert the tool into your drill chuck and clamp it tight.

Cut a 2" piece of pipe cleaner and slide it into the groove cut into the tool shaft. Follow Steps 3 to 6 (left page) to polish the wheel bore.

CHAPTER 8
ASSEMBLY

This is the last step to get your car ready to race. You've got to get all your finely honed parts attached to each other!

This chapter contains many final speed tips. In order for your car to be as fast as it can be, you have to assemble the axles, wheels, and car body properly. You also need to lubricate all the surfaces that will rub together. And of course, the alignment of the wheels must be right. Build a test track to try out your car and get everything set up just perfectly.

ASSEMBLY TOOLS

Grab the stuff shown on this page so you can assemble your Pinewood Derby car.

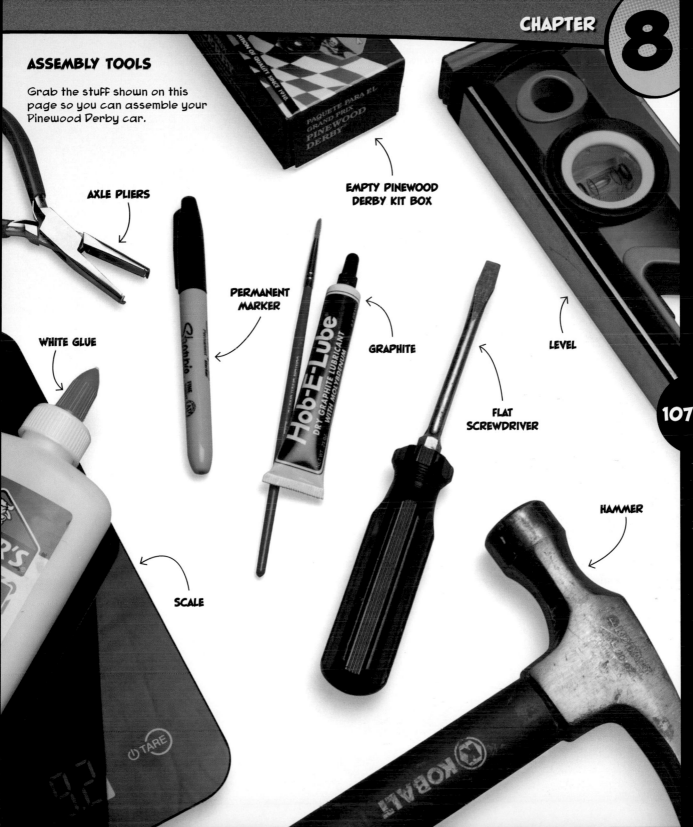

AXLE PLIERS

EMPTY PINEWOOD DERBY KIT BOX

PERMANENT MARKER

WHITE GLUE

GRAPHITE

LEVEL

FLAT SCREWDRIVER

SCALE

HAMMER

ASSEMBLY

STEP 1 - WHEEL LUBRICATION

This is the first step to assembling your rocket-fast car. In this step, we will be applying graphite to all the friction-prone surfaces of the wheels. You will need a soft cloth, soft pipe cleaner, and graphite of your choice.

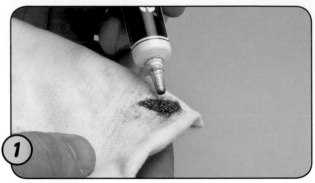

1

Preparing the graphite.
Place a small amount of graphite on the corner of a clean, soft cloth.

2

Applying graphite to the inside rim.
Roll the inside rim of the wheel on the graphite pile. Apply light pressure to buff the graphite onto the edge. Continue buffing the edge until it's shiny and smooth. Repeat for the remaining three wheels.

3

Applying graphite to the wheel hub.
Rub graphite onto the hub and apply light pressure to buff the graphite until the hub is smooth and shiny. Repeat for the remaining three wheels.

4

Preparing to apply graphite to the wheel bore.
Cover a soft pipe cleaner with graphite.

5

Applying graphite to the wheel bore.
Insert the pipe cleaner into the wheel bore and buff the wheel bore until it's shiny. Repeat for the remaining three wheels.

STEP 2 - BODY LUBRICATION

In this step we will be applying graphite to the area around the axle hole. You may want to cover your paint job on the sides of the body with painter's tape to protect it from getting covered in graphite. It's great for lubricating, but graphite it can really mess up a paint job.

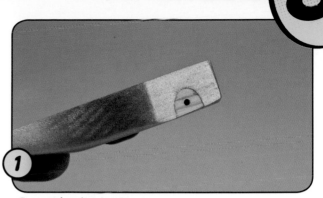

Preparing the body.
If your car is any color other than silver, you will want to protect the paint around the axle hole with painters tape.

Applying the graphite.
Place a small amount of graphite on the corner of a clean, soft cloth and rub it onto the area around the axle hole.

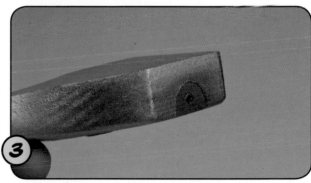

Buff until shiny.
Buff the graphite until the side of the car is shiny.

LUBRICATION OPTIONS

There are a few different types of lubricants available. Below are examples of the most popular types:

Dry graphite - This has been the favorite for many years. It's cheap and easy to find.

Custom graphite mixes - Many of the Web sites selling Derby supplies have their own custom blends of graphite.

Krytox GPL 100 – Using oil lubrication is gaining in popularity. Krytox GPL 100 is very easy to apply, it's not messy, and it will last though all your heat races and still be going strong in the final races. Be sure to check your local rules before you use liquid lubrication.

109

STEP 3 - ATTACHING THE WHEELS

In Step 3, we're finally attaching the wheel for the first time. You will be removing and reinstalling the wheels and axles several times over the next few steps.

Gather your materials.
You will need a pair of scissors, the cardboard from the empty kit box (or cardboard from a cereal box), and painters tape.

110

Making a wheel spacer.
Cut two pieces of cardboard from the empty kit box, about 2" x 3".

Taping the spacer together.
Use painter's tape to tape the two pieces of cardboard together along the sides. Using scissors, cut off the end of the spacer to create an even edge. Cut a slot ⅛" wide by ¼" deep into this edge.

Install the wheels.
Place an axle into a wheel and firmly press the axle into the axle hole. Do not use a hammer. Use the spacer to correctly set the gap between the wheel in the car body. The back end of a Sharpie marker makes a great tool to press against the axle head.

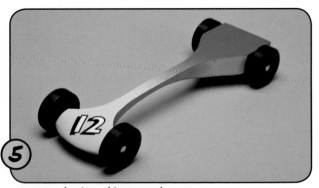

Now it's looking like a real racecar.

STEP 4 - SETTING UP A TEST SURFACE

Ok, so now we need a track... well sort of. Last time I checked an official Pinewood Derby track cost a lot of money, so that option is out. What we need is a smooth clean surface to test our car. The dining room table will work perfectly. We will need a flat area to set the rear alignment and a slightly angled surface to set the steering alignment. Be sure to place a folded towel at the end of the angled surface to stop your car from falling to the ground and breaking into pieces!

Gather the materials.
Grab an extra table leaf and raise it about 2½" on one end. You'll also need painter's tape and something to soften the car's landing.

Apply tape.
Use the painter's tape to make a track about 5" wide the whole way down the leaf.

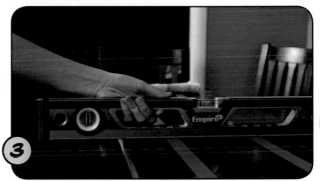

Level the leaf.
Use a level to make sure the leaf is level from side to side. Use folded paper to make adjustments.

THE DERBY WORX PRO-AXLE GUIDE

This tool helps you correctly insert axles into the basic axle slots if you chose or are required to use the slots without any modifications like we made on page 43.

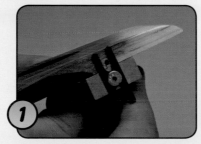

Fit the grooved side of the Pro-Axle Guide into the axle slot as shown in the photo. The metal tabs on the tool are designed to correctly set the gap between the wheel hub and the body.

Firmly hold the tool against the bottom of the car and insert the wheel and axle into the slot.

BUILDING YOUR OWN TEST TRACK!

Here are plans for a test track if you want the perfect surface to set up your car. Store-bought tracks can be very expensive but this track can be built using off-the-shelf parts from your local home center. You can build it in under an hour using basic tools. In the example below, I've built a 16-foot track. You could build an 8-foot track or you can add many 8-foot sections together and build a full 40-foot track.

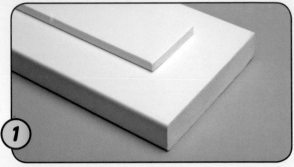

1

Start with one piece of PVC lattice strip, ¼" x 1½" x 8', and one piece of PVC trim plank, ¾" x 3½" x 8'.

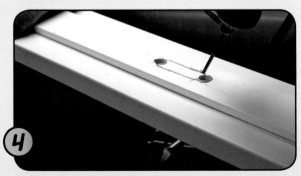

2

Mark center lines on both boards and screw them together with ½" lath screws. Any ½" screw with a wide head will work. Space the screws 24" apart down the boards.

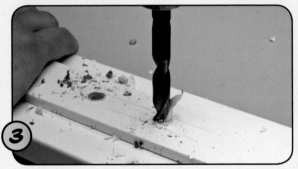

3

Use the drawing on page 115 to determine the location of the slot. Drill a ⅜" hole at both ends of the slot.

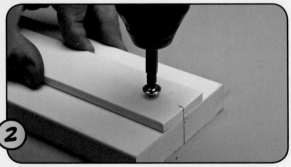

4

Use a coping saw to remove the material between the two ⅜" holes.

5

Use a file or sandpaper to clean up the area around the hole. The hole doesn't need to be perfect.

6 This is the hardware you will need to build a spring-loaded starting gate. The complete list of materials is on page 115.

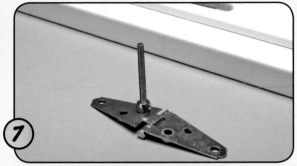

7 With the flat part of the strap hinge facing up, insert the 8-32 x 1¾" Machine Screw into the hole noted in the drawing on page 115. Use a 8-32 Nylon Lock Nut to hold the screw (starting pin) in place.

8 Use the drawing on page 115 to location the position of the strap hinge. Place one #8 flat washer under each hole of the strap hinge and screw it in place.

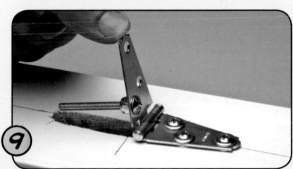

9 Move the hinge up and down to test that it can freely move without hitting the sides of the slot.

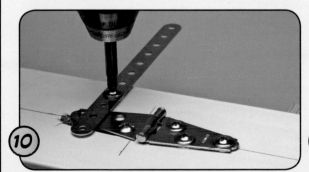

10 Position the ½" x 5½" mending plate in place to hold the strap hinge in its open position. Place two #8 flat washers under the pivot hole and screw it in place. Don't screw it down too tight or the mending plate won't be able to pivot. This mending plate will be the trigger to start the car down the track.

11 Attach one end of the spring to the strap hinge. See the drawing on page 115.

113

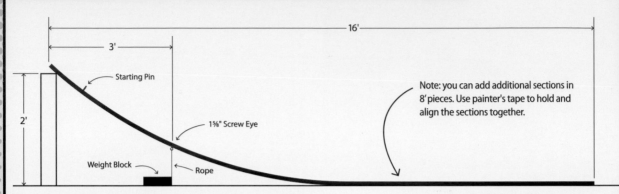

16'

3'

2'

Starting Pin

1⅝" Screw Eye

Weight Block — ← Rope

Note: you can add additional sections in 8' pieces. Use painter's tape to hold and align the sections together.

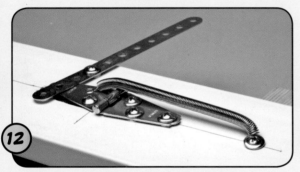

12 Stretch the spring and attach it to the bottom of the track.

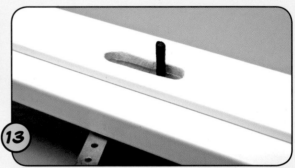

13 Wrap the threads of the bolt with electrical tape to protect the front of your cars.

14 Attach a #8 1⅝" screw eye to the bottom of the track. See the drawing on page 115 for the correct location. Tie a three-foot length of rope to the screw eye. Prop one end of the track about two feet off the ground. Pull the rope down toward the ground and place a heavy object on top of the rope to give the track a smooth bend.

15 Place a towel at the end of the track to stop the car. Swing the starting pin up through the track and rotate the mending plate over the hinge to hold the starting pin in an upright position. Set a car behind the starting pin and rotate the trigger counter-clockwise to release the car.

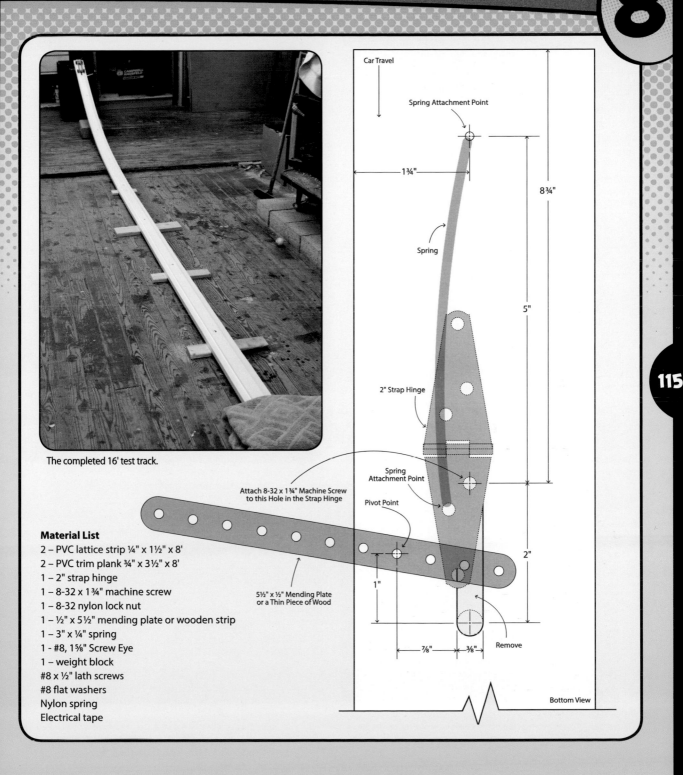

The completed 16' test track.

Car Travel

Spring Attachment Point

1¾"

8¾"

Spring

5"

2" Strap Hinge

Spring
Attachment Point

Attach 8-32 x 1¾" Machine Screw
to this Hole in the Strap Hinge

Pivot Point

2"

Material List

2 – PVC lattice strip ¼" x 1½" x 8'
2 – PVC trim plank ¾" x 3½" x 8'
1 – 2" strap hinge
1 – 8-32 x 1¾" machine screw
1 – 8-32 nylon lock nut
1 – ½" x 5½" mending plate or wooden strip
1 – 3" x ¼" spring
1 - #8, 1⅝" Screw Eye
1 – weight block
#8 x ½" lath screws
#8 flat washers
Nylon spring
Electrical tape

5½" x ½" Mending Plate
or a Thin Piece of Wood

1"

7⅞"

⅜"

Remove

Bottom View

STEP 5 - BENDING AXLES

Now it's time to start the alignment process. In this step, we will be putting small bends into the axles to give our wheels a slight angle, or what is called "canting." The rear wheels will have a canting angle of 2.5 degrees and the fronts will be 1.5 degrees. Canting the wheels has a few advantages as compared to using flat axles. First, only part of the wheel's tread surface will be touching the track. Second, the canting will cause the wheel to rise against the axle head and not bounce back and forth between the axle head and the car body. At this point we have polished the wheel and axle head the friction will be minimal. Last, but not least, the bends in the axles will allow you to make adjustments to the toe-in and toe-out of the wheels. This will allow you control how the car rolls down the track.

Marking the axle shaft.
Insert an axle into a wheel and use a permanent marker to make a mark all around the axle about ⅛" of an inch behind the wheel hub.

Marking the axle head.
Place a mark from the center of axle head to the edge.

Place the axle into a bench vise.
Insert the axle into a bench vise to the line on the axle shaft.

Bending the axle.
Place a flathead screwdriver at the base of the axle, and rest it on the bench vise. Very lightly tap the end of the screwdriver with a hammer.

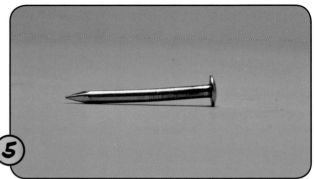

Correctly bent axle.
The axle above is a rear axle that is bent to 2.5 degrees. Use the bending guides on the next page to check and make sure your axles are bent correctly. It's a good idea to practice on a few unused axles first.

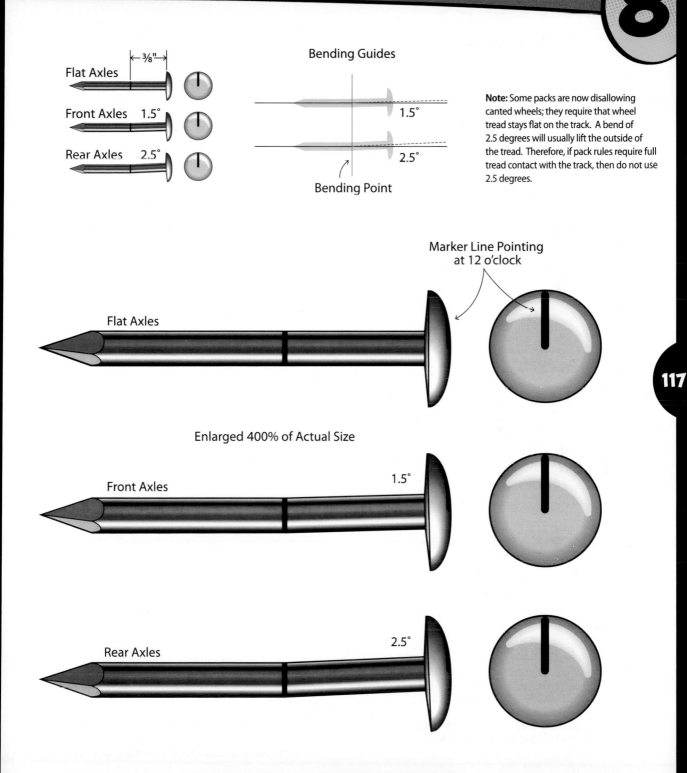

Flat Axles

← ³⁄₈" →

Front Axles 1.5°

Rear Axles 2.5°

Bending Guides

1.5°

2.5°

Bending Point

Note: Some packs are now disallowing canted wheels; they require that wheel tread stays flat on the track. A bend of 2.5 degrees will usually lift the outside of the tread. Therefore, if pack rules require full tread contact with the track, then do not use 2.5 degrees.

Marker Line Pointing at 12 o'clock

Flat Axles

Enlarged 400% of Actual Size

Front Axles 1.5°

Rear Axles 2.5°

117

STEP 6 - REAR WHEEL ALIGNMENT

Now that you have the axles bent to the correct angles, we can reinstall them into the car body. Be sure to install the axles with the mark on the axle head pointing to 12 o'clock. In this step, we will be working on the rear wheels to get them to roll correctly down the track. The goal is to have the rear wheels roll toward the axle head and stay there as soon as the car starts to roll. We don't want the rear wheels to float back and forth between the axle head and the body. As the wheel hits the axle head or the car body, it causes extra friction and slows the car down.

Test surface.
We will need a flat and level test surface where we can roll the car back and forth.

Left rear wheel alignment.
Work on one wheel at a time. Move the car forward and watch the gap between the car body and the wheel hub of the left rear wheel. Does the wheel move to the left and rest against the axle head? Does it move to the right and rub against the car body? Use the diagram on the next page to make small adjustments to the rotation of the axle head and repeat the test until the wheel rolls to the axle head and stays there.

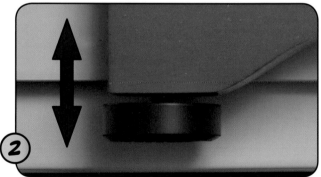

Right rear wheel alignment.
Repeat the same process as the left wheel. Once the right wheel is rolling correctly, test them both at the same time. They should both move toward the axle head at the same time.

Top View

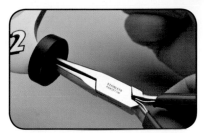

Axle extraction pliers

Axle extraction pliers are available, which are designed to grip the edges of the axle without damaging the wheels or the axle. They allow you to make fine adjustments without removing the wheel or axle.

Left Rear.

If the left rear wheel slides toward the body of the car, rotate the axle clockwise a few degrees. Retest the car on your test surface and continue to adjust the angle until the wheel rests against the axle head rolling the car forward and backward.

Right Rear.

If the right rear wheel slides toward the body of the car, rotate the axle counter-clockwise a few degrees. Retest the car on your test surface and continue to adjust the angle until the wheel rests against the axle head rolling the car forward and backward.

If the left wheel slides toward the car...

If the right wheel slides toward the car...

...rotate the axle clockwise.

...rotate the axle counter-clockwise.

Note: Make the smallest adjustment necessary to get the wheels to track correctly. If you're too aggressive with the axle rotation, you will cause unnecessary toe-in or -out and that can cause a loss of speed.

Rear Wheels Canted 2.5°

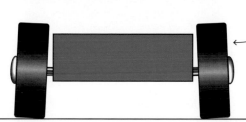

Rear View

STEP 7 - FRONT WHEEL ALIGNMENT

STRAIGHT RUNNER

There are two options for the front wheel alignment. You can set up the car to go straight down the track, known as a "straight runner," or align it so it steers into the center guide, known as a "rail rider." Setting your car to go straight down the track is the best option when your track doesn't have a center guide or if the center guide has rough edges. Your goal is to get your car down the track by striking the center guide the fewest times as possible. Every time your car strikes the center rail, it's losing speed.

Find the wheel that steers.
Place the car on a flat surface. Put your finger on the front center. As you push down, the car will shift toward one of the wheels. The other wheel carries the weight of the front of the car and is known as the steering wheel and steering axle. Remember which wheel is the steering wheel. It's important for the next step.

Make a test run.
Have your car travel down a slightly inclined test surface. Watch your car from the back. Unless you're very lucky, the car will pull to one side or the other. Use the notes on pages 121 to make adjustments to the rotation of the steering axle. Make very small adjustments until your car is traveling straight down the center of the track.

If your car curves left.
Rotate your steering axle counter-clockwise.
See the top illustration on the next page.

If your car goes straight.
Don't touch a thing! You're ready to go!

If your car curves right.
Rotate your steering axle clockwise.
See the bottom illustration on the next page.

If your car curves left...

...Rotate the axle counter-clockwise. This will tilt the axle bend forward, causing the car to steer right.

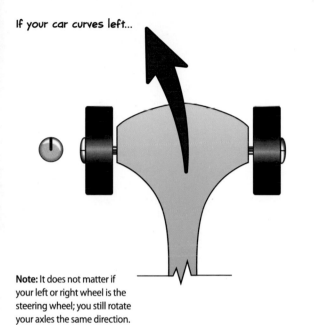

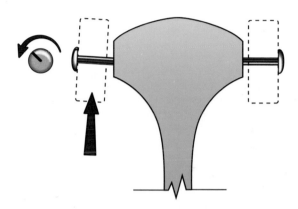

Note: It does not matter if your left or right wheel is the steering wheel; you still rotate your axles the same direction.

If your car curves right...

...Rotate the axle clockwise. This will tilt the axle bend backward, causing the car to steer left.

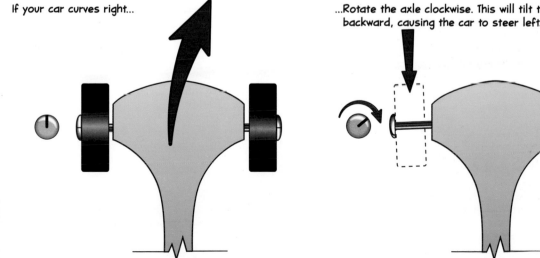

ASSEMBLY

STEP 7 - FRONT WHEEL ALIGNMENT

RAIL RIDER™

The second option for front wheel alignment is a technique is called "Rail Riding™." Credit goes to Jay Wiles for recently popularizing the technique, and for coining the term.

The idea of rail riding is to have your car steer slightly to the center rail within the first few feet of the race. Your car will hug the center rail the entire way down the track, avoiding the back and forth motion that robs speed from your car. You will have friction from the front wheel touching the center rail, but we have already polished the inside rim of the wheel so friction will be minimal.

Use the steering technique on page 121 to adjust the steering of your steering wheel and axle to achieve the proper steering drift.

See page 125 for more information on a tool built to help set up your car for rail riding.

122

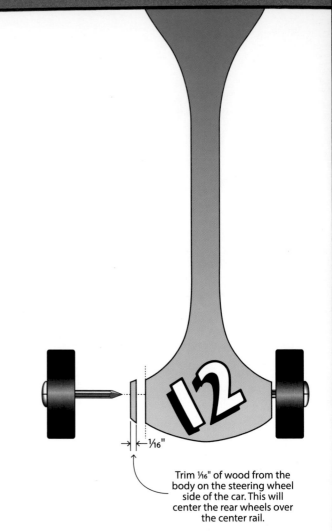

1/16"

Trim 1/16" of wood from the body on the steering wheel side of the car. This will center the rear wheels over the center rail.

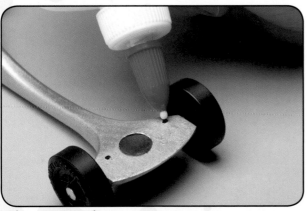

Gluing in the axles.
After the alignment is all set, place a small dab of white glue into the axle gluing holes. Allow the glue to dry overnight. Do not use thin glue such as Super Glue. Thin glues could travel down the axle shaft and get on the polished axle shaft, ruining all your hard work.

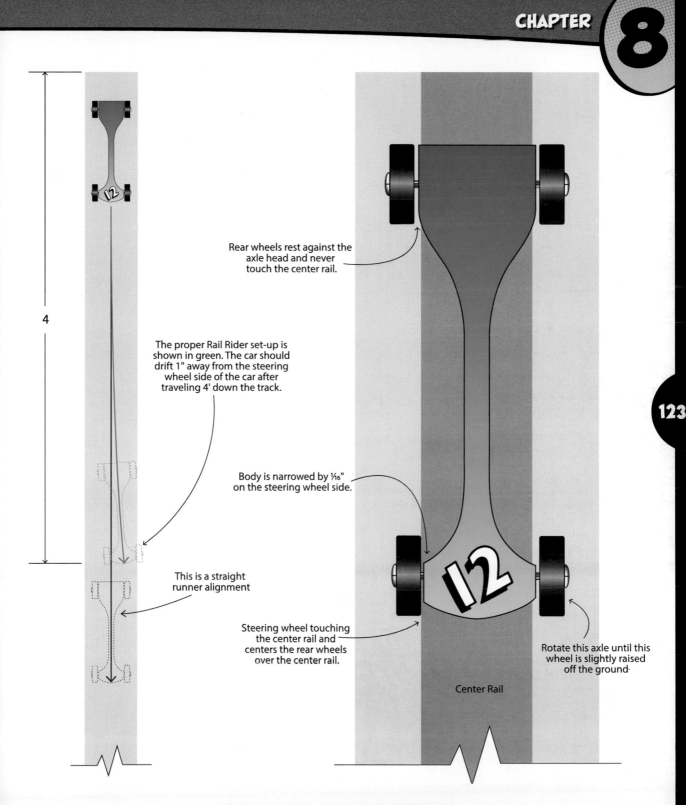

4

Rear wheels rest against the axle head and never touch the center rail.

The proper Rail Rider set-up is shown in green. The car should drift 1" away from the steering wheel side of the car after traveling 4' down the track.

Body is narrowed by ¹⁄₁₆" on the steering wheel side.

This is a straight runner alignment

Steering wheel touching the center rail and centers the rear wheels over the center rail.

Rotate this axle until this wheel is slightly raised off the ground.

Center Rail

STEP 8 - FINAL WHEEL LUBRICATION

Now that we have finished the alignment of the wheels, we can focus on the final preparations before the big race. The first step is to apply the final coating of graphite to the wheels and axles. You don't want to pack the wheels full of graphite. You will get the best performance with a thin coating of graphite.

Gather your materials.
It is easier to get the graphite into the correct locations if you use a small paintbrush. Pour out a small amount of graphite onto a piece of paper and coat the tip of the brush.

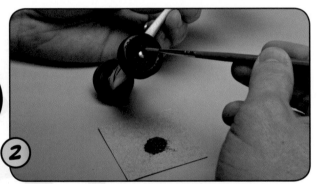

Placing graphite in the outer wheel hub.
Using the tip of the paintbrush, work a small amount of graphite under the head of the axle. Rotate the wheel to work the graphite in.

Placing graphite in the inter wheel hub.
Work graphite onto the wheel hub and down into the wheel bore. Do not pack graphite into the wheel bore.

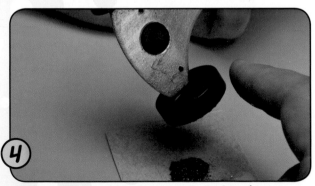

Working the graphite deeper into the wheel bore.
Lightly tap the wheel to help the graphite settle into the wheel bore.

Spinning the wheel.
Slowly spin the wheel to work the graphite around the axle. Spinning the wheel fast will cause the graphite to fly out of the wheel bore. A small amount of graphite will be worked into the surface of the wheel bore.

THE DERBY WORX PRO-RAIL RIDER TOOL

This tool is designed to help you bend your axles to the correct angle. One side of the tool will bend an axle 1.5 degrees and the other side 2.5 degrees. To use this tool you must also have a Pro-Axle Press to hold the axle. Be sure to polish your axles before you use this tool.

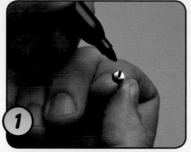

1. Draw a line on the heads of your axles from the center of the axle head to the edge.

2. Place your axle on the Pro Axle Press with the mark facing the 6 o'clock position (down).

3. Put the top on the Pro-Axle Press and allow the axle to stick out ½".

4. Decide if you want a 1.5 or 2.5 degree bend in your axle.

5. Place the correct end of the Rail Rider tool over the top of the Pro-Axle Press.

6. Slide the axle into the Pro-Axle Press until the head of the axle is resting against the Rail Rider tool.

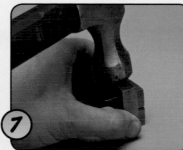

7. Firmly press the axle head against the Rail Rider tool and tap the top of the Rail Rider tool lightly two or three times with a hammer. This will bend the axle to the degree chosen.

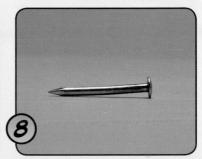

8. Repeat the process for the other three axles. Be sure to bend two axles at 1.5 degrees and two axles at 2.5 degrees.

125

STEP 9 - BURNISHING THE WHEELS

You can continue to refine the thin coating of graphite between the wheel, axle, and the car body by spinning the wheel and burnishing the graphite into the surface of these areas. This should be done with your fingers. You want the wheel to spin the same direction as it would when the car travels down the track.

Position #1.
Hold the car flat like it would travel down the track. Use your finger to spin the wheel. Allow the wheel to spin for 10 to 20 seconds. Continue the process a few more times. Repeat this process for the remaining three wheels.

Position #2.
Hold the car on it side so the wheel hub rubs against the body of the car. Use the same technique as Step #1 to spin the wheels.

Position #3.
Hold the car on the other side so the outer wheel hub rubs against the under side of the axle head. Again, use the same technique as Step #1 to spin the wheels.

STEP 10 - FINAL WEIGHTING

Now, it's time for setting the final weight. The rules allow a car to be a maximum of 5.0 ounces. You want your car to be as heavy as the judges at the check-in station will allow. Have your car weight up to 4.9 ounces before you bring it to the check-in station. Slowly add small pieces of trim weight, see page 67, until the scale reads 5.1 ounces. Then remove very small pieces until the scale says 5.0 ounces.

Weighing the car.
Place your car on the scale and measure out the maximum trim weight you can add.

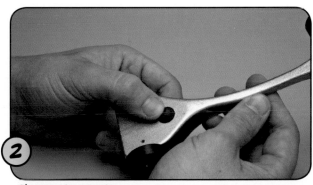

Placing the weight.
Work the trim weight into the hole we previously drilled into the bottom of the car. See page 47.

Balancing the car.
Trim weight can also be added to the hole in the front of the car if you need to fine-tune the center of balance. See page 67 for more details.

The finished car.
At this point your car should read 5.0 on the scale but, in reality, it's 5.04 ounces. Remember, every little thing helps to get the maximum speed out of your car.

CHAPTER 9
RACE DAY

Good luck at the race! Here are a few things to keep in mind, but most of all, be sure to have fun!

Your car has been shaped to perfection. The axles are shiny and smooth; the wheels are round and slick; the weights are perfectly balanced to give the most potential energy at the start of the race. It is decorated to the max, and there's no other car out there that looks as good. You've corrected all the steering problems and made sure everything is ship-shape and ready for the race. Well, now is the big day! This chapter will tell you everything you need to know to get through race day and have a great experience. Read on for the last few secrets you need, and good luck!

RACE DAY SUPPLIES

There are a few things you need to bring with you on Pinewood Derby race day.

MONEY FOR SNACKS

CAMERA

GRAPHITE

SUPER GLUE FOR ANY REPAIRS

TUNGSTEN PUTTY

THIS BOOK TO RECORD YOUR RACE TIMES

129

PERMANENT MARKER TO WRITE YOUR NAME ON THE CAR

PEN TO WRITE YOUR RACE TIMES

TAPE FOR ANY REPAIRS

BE PREPARED

Bring a small tool kit with you to the race. You never know what is going to happen, and you should be prepared. You may even be able to help out a fellow racer.

WHAT WE BRING TO THE RACE:

☐ Graphite
☐ Tungsten putty
☐ Permanent marker
☐ Tape for repairs
☐ Super glue
☐ Money for snacks
☐ Camera
☐ This book and a pen to record your times

CLEAN HANDS

Make sure your hands are clean before holding your car, especially if you just ate a donut! All that sticky stuff will mess up your wheels and make your car run slower.

HOLDING THE CAR

Don't hold your car by the wheels. Hold it by the center. You don't want to mess up all the work you just did to get the wheels rolling super-fast!

NOT A TOY–YET

Never roll your car on any surface before the race-especially the floor. Dirt will stick to your wheels and slow your car down. Wait until after the races are over before you play with your car!

LINE IT UP

When you put your car on the track to race, make sure the wheels are completely in the lane and not sitting up on the lane guides. If not, your car could crash during the race. Also, after your car is on the track, pull your wheels out to the axle heads.

GRAPHITE

Bring graphite or lube, just in case. If you drop the car, or get the wheels dirty, you might be able to clean off the wheels and make the wheel/axle meeting place slippery again. Plus, I always like to have stuff on hand to help other racers. Maybe some of your friends don't know about using graphite, and you can help them out.

SUPERGLUE TO THE RESCUE

Having superglue with you is always a good idea. You never know if something is going to fall off, or if a friend's car might fall apart. You can save the day, with the help of superglue!

STORAGE

Store your finished car in a gallon-size resealable bag to keep your wheels clean. Then, place the bag into a padded shoebox for transportation to the race.

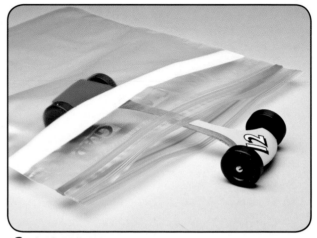

Protect your car.
Seal your car inside of a gallon-sized freezer bag. The bag will protect your car from getting anything inside of the wheel bores.

Wow! If you've never seen a derby racing track before, your first thought will probably be something like..."Wow, that's long!" It's the perfect place to race the cars you just made, and it's a lot of fun to watch.

Place a photo of your finished derby car

Race Details:
Date _____

Location _____

Number of competitors _____

Race Car Details:
Car Number _____

How long did it take to build? _____

Favorite detail on your car _____
_____

Finishing positions:
Race #1 _____

Race #2 _____

Race #3 _____

Finals _____

Favorite memory:
_____
_____
_____
_____

RACE #1			
Lane Number	Lane # 1	Lane # 2	Lane # 3	Lane # 4
Time				
Position				

RACE #2			
Lane Number	Lane # 1	Lane # 2	Lane # 3	Lane # 4
Time				
Position				

RACE #3			
Lane Number	Lane # 1	Lane # 2	Lane # 3	Lane # 4
Time				
Position				

Did you advance to the Final Round? ❑ Yes ❑ No

FINAL ROUND			
Lane Number	Lane # 1	Lane # 2	Lane # 3	Lane # 4
Time				
Position				

Index

Cover and layout designer: Troy Thorne **Editor:** Kerri Landis **Illustrator:** Jason Deller
Step-by-step hand models: Kerri Landis, Nathan Thorne, Kelsey Thorne, and Troy Thorne **Step-by-step photographer:** Scott Kriner

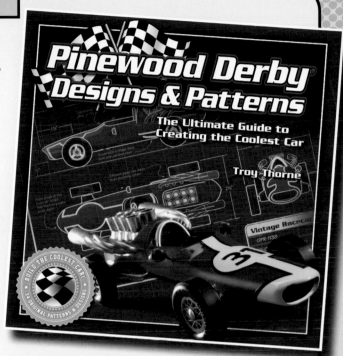

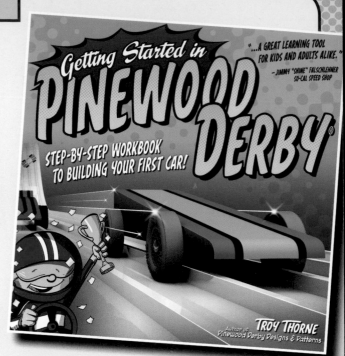